# Myrtle Fillmore: Lighting the Way

## Neal Vahle

# Open View Press

659 14th Avenue
San Francisco, California, 94118
415-831-2455

Printed in the United States of America
ISBN-13: 978-1-4675-4378-1

Design and layout by Eleanor Farrell

# Table of Contents

# Acknowledgements

Several people involved with Unity, many of them Unity ministers, read the manuscript, provided helpful comments, and wrote endorsements which enable potential readers to see the benefits from reading it. They are: Richard Billings, Robert Brumet, Howard E. Caesar, Sharon Connors, Bill and Marge Dale, Justin Epstein, Stan Hampson, John Knowles, Glenn Mosley, Phil Pierson, Rosemary Fillmore Rhea, Michael Sheets, Thomas Shepherd, John Strickland, Paul Tenaglia, Tom Thorpe, Duke Tufty and Philip White.

Michael Maday, after providing counsel on each of the chapters, and endorsing the book, agreed to write the Preface. Maday writes passionately about the contribution of Myrtle Fillmore and tells why, for over a century's time, she has been an inspiration to people both inside and outside Unity.

I thank my friend Jan Adkins for important help in writing Chapter One, "Portrait in Sepia," and for other editorial suggestions. I also thank him for suggestions on the design of the book. I thank my neighbor, Eleanor M. Farrell for designing both the text and cover, and for the layout of the book. I thank Eric Page, the Unity School archivist, for help in obtaining photographs.

Finally, I thank my wife, Nancy Scotton, for proof reading the text. She saved the author from several embarrassing mistakes. I also acknowledge her for the daily encouragement and emotional support that sets the context for my work as a writer. Writing—an isolating and lonely task— is made possible for me by the loving care that she continually provides.

# *Preface*

*By Michael A. Maday*

**M**yrtle and Charles Fillmore, Unity's co-founders, did not believe in celebrating themselves, or in establishing anything like a cult of the personality. If they had, we no doubt would see statues of them at historical spots at Unity Village, the world headquarters for the Unity Movement. I have to admit, however, that I've had my moments of asking if that would have been so bad?

Even so, the Fillmores did have a profound Truth in mind, that they were pointers of the way, not masters themselves. Or to put it another way, they were celebrating the divinity within each of us, and it would not do to have them put themselves up on a pedestal to worship.

Yet we humans can't help but be curious who these giants were, how they lived, why they felt led to reach so far when the vast majority of us are content with what little we find. Or if we are discontented, we don't seek deep into the living matrix of consciousness for our answers, like they did. Yet we are all fed by their search, and by what they found.

So this is the story of Mary Caroline Page, who came to accept the nickname "Myrtle," and then the surname Fillmore from her eventual husband Charles. Their stories are told in this book, how they met, how they became great friends, and correspondents, then married each other, and became pioneers of a new worldwide spiritual movement.

Myrtle was a teacher and a childhood mystic who felt a oneness with God long before she knew the right words to use. She also had a way with people, and with children, teaching for several years in Clinton, Missouri, with a grace that surprised their parents, so much so that they didn't want her to leave. Charles was a businessman and not really religious but who came to view his wife with fascination as he saw her transformed by her healing and by her faith.

It is almost a cliché in Unity circles to consider Charles the "head" and Myrtle the "heart" of the movement. There is a lot to be said for that given how intellectual much of what Charles wrote is, not to mention how this designation fits neatly with Unity's metaphysical ideas of "man" meaning mind, and "woman" feelings or heart. Yet it must be said that Myrtle had quite a mind of her own, and it was the teacher in her that first convinced Charles she was the woman for him, and then convinced him that spirituality had a life far beyond the ritualistic notions so prevalent in nineteenth century America. She had an open mind, and like Charles, devoured ideas from Shakespeare to James Russell Lowell to Ralph Waldo Emerson. Together they went on to explore the cutting edge ideas of their time, in Transcendentalism, Theosophy, Hinduism, Christian Science and the New Thought ideas of Warren Felt Evans. They came to found a new eclectic mix of the best of them all, and called it "Unity."

So Charles showed quite a lot of heart to be so open to his wife, and to keep his mind open to the mind-stretching ideas that came to both of them through their studies with Emma Curtis Hopkins, the great "teacher of teachers," whose writings also reflect the teachings of Ralph Waldo Emerson. Charles began to adopt and explore the radical ideas of healing his wife used to free herself from tuberculosis, and began to grow his withered leg, a medical impossibility.

Today HeartMath, that movement that is exploring how the heart affects mental clarity, creativity, and emotional balance, tells us that the most profound aspect of mind is found in our hearts. Charles demonstrates that in his own way, as does Myrtle, in hers.

Neal Vahle, our biographer, here has given us another glimpse into the lives of Myrtle and Charles. He had already written about them, as well as the entire Unity movement, in his previous books. He tells us in his Introduction why he chose not to reprint *Torchbearer to Light the Way: The Life of Myrtle Fillmore* when it went out of print in 2011, and chose instead to revisit Myrtle's life and give us a fresh biography. Neal feels a sacred bond with Myrtle that I hope he doesn't mind me sharing. I'm glad he wrote this new book because it has motivated me to plunge once more into the stream of ideas that brought Unity to fruition.

At a time when Unity's teachings seem to have become unclear, at least to some, or perhaps submerged under the tidal forces of trying to be too much to too many, this concise, new biography is refreshing. Myrtle Fillmore, the "Mother of Unity," comes alive in this new book. I have felt moved to get to know, on a deeper level, what drove her and her husband to pioneer this new spiritual movement. It excites to me to read how their emphasis on "Practical Christianity" and "Christian healing" inspired this new "Way" of following the teachings of Jesus Christ. It is my prayer that this book rekindles a new commitment to this "household of faith," and empowers clarity and new life for the Unity movement.

*Rev. Michael A. Maday, M.A, is an adjunct professor for Unity Institute and Seminary and former editor for Unity House and Unity Books*

# Introduction

I was relatively new to Unity when I wrote *Torch-Bearer to Light the Way: The Life of Myrtle Fillmore*. I had attended Unity church services in Washington DC, in the 1980s, but had never dug deeply into the Unity teaching until I came to Unity School in 1993 with the intention of writing a biography of Charles Fillmore. When I read Myrtle Fillmore's 1,500 plus letters in the Unity Archives, written between 1928 and 1931, I got a much better grasp of the basic Unity teaching than from reading the works of Charles. I decided at that time to postpone a biography of Charles and write a biography of Myrtle. *Torch-Bearer to Light the Way*, completed in 1995, was the result.

In 1996, I began working on *The Unity Movement: Its Evolution and Spiritual Teaching*, which was published in 2002. From 2000 to 2005 I served as editor of *Unity Magazine*. After finishing my editorship I returned to the biography of Charles. *The Spiritual Journey of Charles Fillmore: Discover the Power Within* was published in 2008. Through twelve years of research and writing I gained a fuller understanding of the Unity spiritual teaching, and the growth and development of the Unity movement, and more knowledge about the life of Myrtle Fillmore.

When *Torch-Bearer* went out of print in November 2011, it was obvious that it would be better to write a new version of the life of Myrtle Fillmore than reprint *Torch-Bearer*. *Myrtle Fillmore: Lighting the Way* improves on *Torch-Bearer* in several ways. In the opening chapter "Portrait in Sepia," I present an overview of Myrtle's involvement in the Unity movement. It would have been impossible for me to write this overview from my knowledge and understanding of Myrtle when I wrote *Torch-Bearer*.

*Torch-Bearer* lacks a systematic account of the Unity spiritual teaching. Information is in bits and pieces in several chapters. The new version pulls it together in a much more coherent way. Information on the Twelve Powers was left out of *Torch-Bearer* because Myrtle never fully explained it in her letters. I understood the doctrine only after reading the works of Charles when preparing his biography. Included in this new version is information on Myrtle's contribution in developing the doctrine.

Bodily regeneration and reincarnation needed an improved, more succinct presentation. Both were incomplete and somewhat misleading. There are better descriptions of her positions on both in this new work.

*Torch-Bearer* did not give Charles Fillmore full credit for his contribution. The new version provides more detail on how Charles worked with Myrtle in developing the Unity teaching and how organizational abilities enabled Unity to develop and grow.

The description of the development of Silent Unity is much more coherent than in *Torch-Bearer*, as is the information on Myrtle's work as a spiritual counselor, practitioner of spiritual healing, and teacher of Truth Principles at Unity School.

Myrtle's letters indicate that she read widely in the spiritual literature of the day, and that she relied on others for parts of her teachings. *Torch-Bearer* provides only sketchy information about those whose writings she consulted. That been rectified in this new work.

The final chapter of *Torch-Bearer* is entitled "She led the Way." That title is misleading. Parts of the chapter have been re-written to present a more correct view of her contribution.

The chapter on the Fillmore family has been expanded to provide more information on Charles and Myrtle's sons Lowell and Rickert, as well as their grandson, Charles R. Fillmore and great grand-daughter, Connie Fillmore, both of whom served as president of Unity School. The only parts of *Torch-Bearer* that remain untouched are those dealing with the early years of Myrtle and Charles.

# 1
# A Portrait in Sepia

The early 20th Century produced only a handful of strong women who created enterprises that had a major impact on society in America . Those who stand out are Clara Barton, the American Red Cross; Susan B. Anthony, the National Women's Suffrage Association; Mary Baker Eddy, Church of Christ Scientist; and Frances E. Willard, Women's Christian Temperance Union. As co-founder in the Unity School of Christianity, and its prayer ministry, Silent Unity, Myrtle Fillmore ranks with these powerful women.

Silent Unity began in her living room in 1890 when she and her husband Charles began praying with others who joined them each evening from around the country. The prayer ministry grew until by the time of her death 1931, ninety Silent Unity prayer workers were responding to 220,000 prayer requests annually.

In the year 2011, Silent Unity's three hundred prayer workers responded to approximately 1,300,000 annual prayer requests. Under Myrtle's guidance Silent Unity became by 1930 one of the largest prayer ministries in the world, which it continues to be to this day. The work of Silent Unity is called "absent healing." In absent healing the recipient is not present when the healer offers words of prayer. Feedback from those who have benefited from Silent Unity prayer work indicate that their health has been renewed, their relationships restored and their prosperity increased.[1]

The Christianity that Myrtle Fillmore taught and practiced, which is the basis of the Silent Unity work, is radically different from that of Catholicism and Protestantism. She believed that the divine existed within men and women, viewing God as an Indwelling Presence, rather than an all-powerful external Being who must be worshipped. She saw Jesus as a highly evolved human being, conscious of the Indwelling Presence within himself, who set an example for humankind. She did not view Jesus, as much of traditional Christianity views him, as God who came down in human form from heaven to save and redeem humankind from sin. The Unity School of Christianity, which she co-founded, presents this view of the divine in humankind as a part of its teaching today.

Born in 1845, Myrtle grew up in a small Ohio town in what she described as a "Christian atmosphere" among "God-fearing people."

While she was raised in a nurturing family environment, she did not accept the view of God held by her loving mother who believed that if God saw fit to punish his children, he had reason for it.[2]

Myrtle was an avid reader as a young person and exhibited a curious and wide-ranging mind. She was particularly attracted to "the old myths, the fairy tales, histories and scientific works." She believed the visions of scientists had a lot to do with present day life.

Myrtle had a great love of nature and found sustenance in it from the time she was a youth:

> I delighted in getting out in the garden, or to walk in the woods. I loved to touch a tree, and felt that it was truly intelligent. I received something very satisfying from my close contact with Nature. I know, now, that I was feeling and responding to the omnipresent Spirit of God. And that the abundant Life of God was pouring out to me from everywhere, and that my hungry soul and body were drinking it in and rejoicing to express it.[4]

Given her interest in books and learning, it comes as no surprise that Myrtle would be attracted to teaching. After getting a degree from Oberlin College in Ohio she accepted a teaching position in Clinton, Missouri. Myrtle loved teaching and often spoke about the interesting young folks whom it was her privilege to instruct. She said she particularly enjoyed encouraging student interest "in the best literature."[5]

She taught there for thirteen years before going to Denton, Texas for treatment of tuberculosis. It was in Texas that she met her future husband, Charles Fillmore. They were married in 1881 and ultimately settled in Kansas City where he engaged in the real-estate business. Myrtle had continuing bouts with tuberculosis. "I had all the ills of mind and body that I could bear. Medicine and doctors ceased to give me relief and I was in despair.[6] . . . I was supposed to be dying, or very close to it.[7]

A turning point came in 1886 when she attended a series of lectures in Kansas City on spiritual healing given by Dr. E.B. Weeks of the Illinois Metaphysical College. The impact was immediate on Myrtle. She explained, "I had been laboring under the belief in inherited ill health, and the Truth of my divine parentage freed and healed me.[8] To another she wrote:

> You ask what restored me to vigorous health. It was a change of mind from the old, carnal mind that believes in sickness to the Christ Mind of life and permanent health. "Be ye transformed by the renewal of

your mind" (Rom. 12:2). "As he thinketh in his heart, so is he" (Prov. 23:7A.V). I applied spiritual laws effectively, blessing my body temple until it manifested the innate health of spirit.[9]

In 1890 Myrtle and Charles began practicing absent healing in the evening from their home in Kansas City. At the same time they announced the formation of the Society of Silent Help (the name was changed to the Society of Silent Unity in 1891). One of the purposes of the Society was to engage in absent healing. Those who joined, from Kansas City and around the country, were invited to sit with the Fillmores in the silence at 9:00 pm every evening. During this time of silence Myrtle sent out healing affirmations to members of the Society.

Members soon began sending letters with specific requests for healing and prayer support. When the volume of letters got beyond their ability to respond personally, the Fillmores engaged others to help. By 1900 there were three Silent Unity letter-writers responding to members of the Society. By 1911 sixteen healers were answering letters and telegrams. By 1920 Silent Unity had forty prayer workers. In 1930, one year before Myrtle's death, a staff of ninety responded to approximately 200,000 people, mostly subscribers to Unity's six magazines, who contacted them annually by letter or telephone.

Throughout her long career at Unity School, Myrtle spent a good part of the work-day at her desk writing letters to people who had corresponded with her, many of them women, asking for advice on how deal with their lives. Her responses were often took up several pages.

Myrtle was uninhibited in her expression of love for her correspondents. "I am pleased you felt free to write to me," she told a new Unity student:

> I have put you right in my heart, the warmest place I have, so I may bless you with my heart's love, which is really God's love expressing through me as a channel.[10]

Myrtle exuded warmth. She could be particularly loving with women friends who were long-time correspondents. She told Elizabeth:

> Just as I was writing a letter to our blessed Richard one day last week, your cheerful message arrived, together with the one you received from him so I had you there, both of you at once, in my heart's arms. Hearts *do* have arms, you know, as well as eyes and ears and tongues and willing feet. So I just hugged you up close for a while.[11]

She could be critical if her correspondent appeared lost in negative thoughts and emotions:

> **If you were as persistent in carrying out our suggestions of Truth as you are in convincing us of your grief, and sorrow and lack and worry and struggles to find work and supply, you would get on beautifully.**[12]

At the same time she didn't pretend to be perfect, or to be spiritually advanced, acknowledging that she also struggled.

If you are like most of us, and I believe you are, you almost hourly think or do something, or are moved by some impulse, which admits to your unbelief, lack of faith, lack of assurance that God is all in all, and ever shall be in the fullness of good of every kind. But we have the Christ Mind, and are all learning to use it.[13]

She acknowledged that she wasn't always right in giving advice, and that she could mistaken:

> **I feel that you have an apology coming to you, my dear, for my letter of July 27th had not been in the mails long until I felt that my zeal, enthusiasm and desire to help had run away with my better judgment and wisdom in the matter.**[14]

Smoking was a popular pastime in the 1920s. Myrtle was one of the few who found it repulsive and raised objections. She told a friend:

> **I think you will smile when I tell you that our men folks consider me a crank about smoking, and they like to tease me, and make me think I can't go certain places because the folks will be smoking… Someway, I just can't quite see it, that what I call a real Christ-like person would waste time and energy in smoking. I can't quite see the picture of the Christ, with a cigarette or cigar hanging from his mouth, or even between his fingers. I can't see a cloud of enveloping his head, or pouring from his lips, I can't quite imagine him laying a cigarette on the table or tossing it to the ground, before stretching forth his hand to bless and heal one who comes to him in faith.**[15]

Myrtle Fillmore was an active woman. She loved being at Unity School; she loved her work. She preferred being in Kansas City with her fellow Unity workers than going on vacation. She describe her work day in a letter to her sister:

**You'd smile to see me rushing around, trying it keep up with the many things I find myself "in for."... And I just keep getting stronger, and younger and happier and more interested in things than ever.**[16]

At age 83 she was still able to climb stairs and be active into the night. She told a correspondent:

**We climb up and down six flights of winding stairs, several times day! Working all day, and several times a week, far into the evening, and going to bed happy, and eager for the next day.**[17]

She and her husband Charles, co-founder of Unity School, worked well together. Martha Smock, long-time editor of Unity's *Daily Word*, magazine observed their working relationship:

There seemed to be a great deal of understanding and mental and spiritual rapport between these two unique individuals. Each one seemed to encourage the other to be himself and to do his best. They managed to convey a spirit of love and gaiety that has carried forward through the unity work.[18]

At times Myrtle played the dominant role in their partnership, as indicated the testimony of a person who attended the Sunday services they conducted:

For many years Myrtle Fillmore took more than half the time allotted for the Sunday morning lecture. Many times I have sat in the audience and heard Mr. Fillmore remark at the close of her talk that it was time to close the service and that he would just add a few closing remarks for his sermon.[19]

Smock commented on the personal qualities that enabled her to relate well with people at work:

**Myrtle Fillmore had a genius for getting along with people and for drawing the best out of others. She seemed to recognize qualities in people that no one else saw—not even the person themselves... I have talked with people who knew them personally, and with her secretary of the early years, and all of them say the same thing about Myrtle: that she was a gentle, loving, warm person who never pushed herself, who never sought recognition or glory for herself, who never demanded credit for things.**[20]

Myrtle was apparently, not only respected, but well liked by the workers at Unity School. At age 86 she was honored at May Day picnic for workers at Unity farm in June 1931. She told a friend about it:

I was chosen Queen of the May, and was before the floodlights for a while, and now I wouldn't be surprised to receive an offer from Hollywood. Mr. Ingraham, who crowned me, said in his speech that after considering all the candidates for queen they unanimously decided to choose the youngest and the fairest and the most loved—and so I was chosen. It was very sweet and lovely for the workers to pay me such a tribute and I certainly appreciate the spirit of it.[21]

May Rowland, who was a leading figure in the Unity movement for many year had these words of praise:

Myrtle Fillmore was a radically alive person—she had a universal consciousness and a strong family feeling—[and] considered every person a vital part of the work. She felt that everybody who was connected with it, or who wrote to us, or who came to visit headquarters was a part of "our family."... Mrs. Fillmore was a lovable woman, and took everyone she met just as though they were old friends.[22]

# ❧ 2 ❧
# Spiritual Teaching

## Introduction

Beginning in 1890 and continuing for over four decades, Myrtle Fillmore corresponded with men and women, old and young, who wrote to her for spiritual guidance and advice. She corresponded with them for the purpose of teaching them the principles of the Truth of Being. Her correspondence was voluminous. She spent part of every work-day writing letters, and if the last three years of her life are a good measure, she wrote over five hundred letters each year.

This correspondence—many letters are several pages long— reveals an energetic, dedicated, committed, knowledgeable and caring woman. She had a sharp mind and wrote with clarity in responding to her correspondents. The basic Unity teaching comes through more clearly in Myrtles letters than in the books of Charles Fillmore.

## Truth Principles

Myrtle Fillmore's urge to teach grew out of her belief that life was a school for spiritual learning with spiritual awakening the goal. "In this school of experience, she wrote, "we are drilled until we are proficient in our work.[1] We could graduate from the school of life when we understood and applied the principles of the "Truth of Being."

She urged her correspondents to study and put into practice these "Truth Principles"[2] or "Christ Principles," as she sometimes called them. She told a correspondent "Practice the Truth Principles in all the details of daily thinking and living, because these details make up the whole of living."[3] She told another correspondent.

> Through an understanding of Truth principles, and through their application in all the affairs of life, you can come into permanent possession of your Divine inheritance and manifest health, happiness, wisdom and success.[4]

She viewed Truth Principles as all-important:

> There is nothing to compare with understanding of Truth… Truth principles are laws which, when they are understood and followed, will result in peace of mind, health of body and prosperity in affairs.[5]

## The Nature of God

One of the primary "Truth Principles" concerned the nature of God. Myrtle did not view God as a Supreme Being existing separate and apart from humankind. It was wrong to think of God "as a being who is apart from you, and who rewards you according to His 'whim' or according to some particular merit."[1] She told one of her correspondents:

> I am thinking of the difference between our present understanding of God, and the old idea we, some of us, held about God—as though he were a great ruler on a throne, away off somewhere, far above the earth. Personally, I am not interested in a God who is chiefly concerned with the shortcomings of his subjects.[2]

Myrtle viewed God as "everywhere present, as inexhaustible and free as the air we breathe"[3] … in all, through all, above all."[4] Since God is everywhere present, God also resides within humankind. Central to her teaching was the idea that human beings could discover God by turning within themselves:

> God is in you and you are in God"[5] … God and man are one and the same—it is God in us who gives us mind, and life, and love, and substance"[6] … God is actually right within you—as the very Mind which gives you intelligence, the very Life which gives you vitality.[7]

Myrtle was specific in telling a correspondent where not to look for God, and where she might find God:

> Stop looking to a God way off somewhere in the outer, but stand steadfastly in the realization that in God "we live, and move and have our being," and center your attention upon God in the midst of you.[8] … It is for us to go within and develop our souls, and bring our innate resources, capabilities and possibilities into expression.[9]

## Mind and Consciousness

A key element in Myrtle's teaching, and an important Truth Principle, was the idea that the human mind possessed great power. "The mind is powerful and the body and its functions readily and fully do the bidding of the mind."[1] The starting point of all human activity lies in the mind. "All action takes place first in the realm of mind."[2] In passage after passage she wrote about the power of the mind in creating the reality we experience in every day life:

Our affairs are just an extension of our consciousness; as a man thinketh in his heart, so is he in mind, body and affairs"[3] … All man's experiences in the outer world would have their origin in thinking, so that
his outer world corresponds with his consciousness.[4]

Myrtle used the word "consciousness" to describe the states of mind that
humans entered into through thought. She used the metaphor of a house to
describe where consciousness resided. "Our consciousness might be likened
unto a house, and the rooms in the house would symbolize the different states
of mind that have been built up through our thinking."[5] One of the rooms was
occupied by the Christ Consciousness, and another by the Carnal Mind, the
Race Mind and Sense Consciousness.

## Jesus, Traditional Christianity and the Christ Consciousness

Jesus, in Myrtle's view, was "the way-shower." Myrtle indicated, that Jesus,
more than any other man or women, demonstrated the divinity that lay in
potential in all men and women. "Jesus helped humanity, not by giving them
temporal wealth, material things, but by showing them how to find their own
innate divinity."[1] His capacity to serve grew out of his understanding of the
divinity within himself:

> His capacity to give—to bless others with healing, was greater than
> anyone we know of. He developed that ability to give service, as a
> resulting of finding the kingdom of God within.[2]

Myrtle considered it a mistake to view Jesus as traditional Christianity viewed
him. "Instead of thinking of the Lord as the personal Jesus Christ, who is away
at some distant place called heaven," she advised a correspondent, "begin to
think of the Lord as your own God-given Christ-Mind, and Jesus Christ as ever
with you in the spiritual consciousness that he established."[3] The great work of
Jesus was not about helping humans attain heaven after death, but in developing
their spiritual powers. Myrtle indicated, "The Creator put within each soul all
the qualities, ideals and capabilities that will enable us to accomplish the mighty
things that Jesus demonstrated."[4]

Myrtle believed that Traditional Christianity had misinterpreted the teachings of Jesus. As a result, many Christians did not understand "the practical
fundamental principles upon which true religion is based."[5] The gap was wide.
"We as Christian people had thought of Jesus as a splendid standard to go by,
"she declared, "but the churches have failed to live up to His doctrine and life,

and the result is confusion and restlessness, which is not in accord with the promise of Jesus, 'In me ye shall find peace.'"[6]

Myrtle's interpretations of the Scriptures differed in significant ways from those of traditional Christianity, Protestant or Catholic. Myrtle concluded that little credence should be given to the Biblical teachings of traditional Christianity because the Bible had not been correctly translated. "There are hundreds of mistranslations of the King James Bible. We cannot read the Scriptures and interpret them according to the letter." Quoting from Jesus she wrote, "Not of the letter but of the Spirit, for the letter killeth, but the spirit giveth life." Proper use of intuition was necessary for a "true interpretation of the Scriptures." "Spiritual things" are intuitively discerned."[7]

Many of Myrtle's interpretations of Scripture were at odds with traditional Christianity. Her teaching on the nature of God was a prime example. Myrtle made no bones about pointing out the differences. She wrote:

> **Some of the orthodox teachings about God and man's relation to the Creator are so inconsistent that it is quite natural that thinking people should question these things concerning the All Good.[8]… The Church's habit of teaching people about God, as one Presence, the Devil as another presence, and about human beings as another presence, and its failure to teach individuals their oneness with the One Mind, has resulted in superstition.[9]**

Many traditional Christians believed the heaven was a place where you went to after death if you lived a good life. Myrtle did not agree. "Heaven is not a place," she said. "It's a state of mind."[10]

Myrtle believed that the spirituality of Native Americans came closer to divine reality than the traditional Christian teachings:

> **I often think that the Indians' concept of a Great Spirit brought them, nearer to the Creator, than the Christian's concept of a personal God could ever bring civilized man to his God.[11]**

Jesus developed what Myrtle described as the "Christ Mind" or the "Christ Consciousness," through his conscious recognition and inner realization of his oneness with God. Myrtle believed that Jesus had no greater inherent powers than other human beings, and that his accomplishments were within our reach. "He demonstrated his divinity every step of the way, and taught us that what he did all men and women can do."[12]

Myrtle described the importance of raising our consciousness to the level of Jesus:

> The really important thing, you know, is to lift the conscious above things of the material world—above personality and human limitations—and to unfold the Christ consciousness… To do the works that Jesus promised His followers would do, one must raise his consciousness to where [one is] able to see the perfect "image and likeness" in all people.[13]

Myrtle told a correspondent not to look to others to find the Christ, but to look within.

> To live by the Christ pattern does not mean that we seek to conform our individual lives to the ways and teachings of another, but that we respond to the divine impulse within.[14]

Since we have the same innate capabilities as Jesus had, our task in life is to manifest the Christ Consciousness. Myrtle said, "When we think in Christ Consciousness, we do, in all our living habits, that which is quickening, cleansing and strengthening."[15]

Each of us, Myrtle believed, should seek to "build the Christ Consciousness of life into our thoughts, our body consciousness, our very cell structures."[16] Focusing our thought and attention on the Christ within was the key:

> The more you think about your indwelling Christ, the greater will be its expression in you."[17]… When we think in Christ Consciousness, we do, in all our living habits, that which is quickening, and cleansing and strengthening, and powerful in renewing the body in every way.[18]

"The purpose of life," she told a correspondent, "is to find the Christ and live the Christ life."[19]

## The Carnal Mind, The Race Mind, and Sense Consciousness

Myrtle saw carnal consciousness as standing in the way of our attaining Christ Consciousness in our lives. The carnal mind was comprised of negative states of consciousness in which "adverse, selfish, destructive thoughts prevailed." Myrtle described in detail the characteristics of the carnal mind, indicating that people who were dominated by carnal consciousness were not able to manifest the divine within. She told a correspondent:

Understand that when ideas of Truth begin their work in man's consciousness, the carnal mind feels that forces are at work to displace and overrule it. Not clearly discerning the cause of the feeling of insecurity, the carnal consciousness attributes it to the influence of other people, or the stars, or enemies or various other things. The serpent of sense consciousness in the carnal mind is very sly, treacherous, deceiving; it tries to make one believe that there is power if "evil." It tries to make one believe that the realm of appearances is the real world. It is opposed to the Christ Mind, the Truth, and sets up opposition to spiritual things.[1]

Included in the negative states in the carnal mind were greed, prejudice, intolerance, fear, anxiety, hatred, injustice, and confusion. Myrtle characterized the carnal mind's capacity for the demoniac:

The carnal mind is the only devil there is, and of course, it doesn't tend to give up its reign in the individual; so when the Spirit of Truth sends its "angels" of light into human consciousness, the "old devil" of carnal mind does all in its might to destroy the messengers of Truth.[2]

Myrtle indicated that humans experienced a battle going on in their minds between the forces of the Christ Mind and the Carnal Mind.

It is the carnal mind in us that is opposed to the ideas of Truth that try to come into our minds from the Divine Mind. The reason for this is that the carnal mind does not want to give up its dominion to the Christ Mind.[3]

Myrtle acknowledged that it was difficult to overcome the influences of the carnal mind. She counseled:

It takes great strength and courage to break away from carnal bondage, and receive the messages inspired by the Spirit of truth. Unless the soul is strong and positive, and can maintain its hold upon Christ, The Truth, it is apt to suffer adverse experiences that are the result of carnality trying to fight off the Spirit of the Lord and to maintain its dominion over the individual consciousness.[4]

Myrtle attributed the existence of carnal consciousness in many people to the negativity in their early childhood training and to "the telegraphic messages of our parents, our teachers, our playmates, and our pals, and our business associates, and our friends and our superiors, and the world in general."[5]

Myrtle did not believe that the carnal mind would ultimately dominate human consciousness. She saw a continued growth towards the Christ life. She noted:

> Gradually the natural man develops the capacity to express the attributes of the Divine Man, the Christ, and thus transcends bondage to the carnal law.[6]

Another room in Myrtle's mythical house of consciousness was occupied by "race consciousness." The errors of race consciousness included, prejudice, greed, hoardings, and selfishness."[7] She continued:

> As long as you allow old race beliefs in evil, and devil, and lack, and fear, and disease, and other such undesirable things to have place in our mind, you will have some evidence of their outworking in the body.[8]

Myrtle noted that positive thought was needed to deal with the race mind. "By sending forth into the race consciousness your good thoughts and inspired ideas, you help to purify and uplift the sea of race thought."[9]

Sense consciousness had a room of its own in Myrtle's house of consciousness. Those whose lives were focused on he acquisition of material goods found themselves consigned to this room. They would remain there until they had made "certain adjustments" in their consciousness.[10]

> The man who believes in materiality and looks to sense consciousness for satisfaction is clothed in garments of darkness. Every thought has life and substance. When we think about material things and conditions as being real and having power, we give them the life and substance of our thought. When we give our attention to sense consciousness, which deals with material things, we build up the sense man in ourselves; he takes the essence of our souls for himself to the extent that we let our thoughts dwell on things apart from God, the Source.[11]

## *Spiritual Practice*

Spiritual practice was required both to overcome the effects of the carnal mind and to manifest the Christ Consciousness. She urged her correspondents to "practice Truth principles in all the details of daily thinking and living."[1]

These practices included using intuition; disciplining the mind; affirmations; imagery; denials; divine love; prayer; meditation; focusing on the present moment; joy; dream interpretation; persistence; and faith.

Practicing Truth Principles was vitally essential. "Our spiritual ministry is only half done," she explained, "unless we give those unto whom we minister an explanation of the Christ principles that will enable them to demonstrate spiritual laws for themselves."[2]

Myrtle did not assume that because she and her husband Charles spent their lives teaching Truth principles and attempting to practice them, that they were spiritually advanced. She told a correspondent:

> We are here just like other folks. We cannot claim to have proved in our own lives all the Truth that we are learning and that we express in our writings. We are earnestly endeavoring to live the Truth, and to be loving and considerate and practical and happy.[3]

## 1. Using Intuition

For those who sought to manifest the Christ Consciousness it was necessary to develop and use intuition. "Intuition," Myrtle asserted, was "the divine knowing faculty" helping people "know beyond question of doubt" what was their "best good."[1]

It was a faculty that went beyond reason, giving guidance the rational mind was incapable of providing. When we awaken "the knowing faculty of mind-intuition," we no longer need "to stop and reason out seeming conflicts and inconsistencies that appear."[2] She distinguished between the power of the left-brain with the power of intuition with the pithy comment, "Intellect reasons, but intuition knows."[3]

Intuition came from the depths of the human spirit, and constituted the voice of the soul. Myrtle urged her correspondents to use it:

> Those who understand the soul to be the total of consciousness, the fruit of the individual entity's experiences in unfolding and expressing what the Creator has given… realize that these leadings, or voices, which they intuitively know to be right and dependable, come from the innermost realms of the soul itself.[4]

It was important, she believed, to rely on your own inner knowing rather than accept the dictates of outside authorities, particularly in matters of spirit. She advised:

> Now that you have the inner conviction that the only reliable source of instruction is the Spirit of Truth within you, make up your mind that you will stand by this inner leading regardless of the various doctrines that people try to force upon you. Your own intuition will show you whatever degree of truth there may be in all doctrines that come to your attention. When the Mind of Truth within you shows you that thing is true, accept it; do not accept a proposition as true merely because somebody says it is the truth.[5]

Myrtle advised Unity students to rely on their own inner knowing, even it didn't seem to be in accord with Unity spiritual teaching. "Instead of thinking so much about what Unity teaches," she told a correspondent, "cultivate the habit of going directly to the Christ Mind within for your light, your authority. You will find yourself knowing and speaking that which is most helpful and clear."[6]

## 2. Disciplining the Mind

Myrtle told her correspondents that they needed to be aware of when they were harboring negative thoughts and emotions, and take action to shift their consciousness from the negative to the positive. She said, "You must refuse to open the door of your mind to any anxious negative thought. You cannot let these 'thieves and robbers' of your health and peace of mind come in.[1] . . . When the mind is undisciplined and open to all kinds of disagreeable thoughts there can be no peace."[2] She believed that these thoughts could be controlled. She told a correspondent:

> God has given you power to control and discipline your thinking. Exercise this power, dear child of God, and refuse to allow thoughts of sickness and lack to enter your mind. By changing your thinking to conform to the Truths of your Being, you will be transformed.[3]

Disciplining the mind takes constant work, as our minds have the tendency to drop into negative thinking:

> You must discipline your mind day after day, and control your thoughts, so that you will not be full of faith one moment, and doubting, wavering and unstable the next.[4]

## 3. Affirmations

One of the primary ways of shifting consciousness is through the use of affirmations. Affirmations, she said, "are just the right arrangement of words to train the thoughts into harmonious ways."[1] Affirmations that worked well took the form of declarations. "Begin to declare," she told a correspondent, "that you are the strong, healthy, free, wise, powerful, beautiful, successful child of God."[2]

In making declarations of "Truth" the words one chooses are important and should be carefully selected:

> Get the affirmations—which are just the right arrangement of words—fixed in the mind, so that they will automatically discipline any negative or undesirable thoughts or habits that might spring up.[3]

Affirmations should be on our lips as we move through the day. She suggested that you say to yourself, "I am stepping out to face blessings, to face prosperity, to face the glory of life."[4]

Myrtle indicated that "I AM statements of Truth" are particularly effective. "I AM," she asserted, "is God expressing in you, in your mind, in your soul and body."[5] She suggested:

> Instead of letting your thoughts run along old lines of materiality, when you are busy with daily duties, as well as when you pray, use "I AM" truths. Make them an established part of your consciousness. The more you think about "I AM" your Christ self, the greater will be the realization of your innate righteousness and purity.[6]

Myrtle believed that the I AM statements of Jesus are particularly powerful and recommended that we use them:

> I AM the resurrection and the life. I AM the light of the world. I AM with you always. I AM the health of my people. I AM and there is naught beside me. Be still and know that I AM God. I AM that I AM.[7]

## 4. Imagery

Myrtle believed that visual images could have the same positive impact on the mind as affirmations:

> The lamp of the body is the eye, and when you train your spiritual vision to see only perfection, you will behold the ever-present kingdom

of God, and it will become so substantial in your consciousness that it will take form in your body and affairs.[1]

And to another she wrote:

> Erase from your mind the tendency to see lack, and in its place establish the good habit of seeing abundance made manifest. Don't see the bare earth—but with your spiritual eye of faith that beholds God's abundance, see the earth bring forth its bountiful harvest. Apply this idea to everything in your life where fear appears.[2]

Myrtle often backed up her suggestions to her correspondents with examples from her own life. She recalled how she herself had used imagery to overcome a negative condition:

> It occurred to me when meditating, to imagine just how I'd feel if I were freed from the condition. [She didn't indicate the nature of the negative condition] I entered fully into the imagination of freedom and wholeness, Lo! I discovered I was in actual manifestation of all that my imaging faculty declared for me.[3]

## 5. *Denials*

Another way of dealing with negative thoughts is to deny that they have power over us. Myrtle explained how she used them. "In our work," she wrote," we sometimes use denials of an error before proceeding with the quickening, awakening, regenerating Truth."[1] She warned that one had to be careful in using denials. "We don't tell you to deny the existence of seeming problems, or shortcomings. Admit them, if you will... but don't identify yourself with them."[2] Denials were appropriate in a variety of situations. "Deny all belief in weakness, colds, inefficiency—negativity of every kind."[3] She noted that denials were particularly helpful in dealing with fear. "Deny out of both your consciousness and your subconscious, all thought of fear in all its phases along every line."[4]

## 6. *Divine Love*

Manifesting the Christ Consciousness is not possible, Myrtle explained, without making "conscious at-one-ment with the universal, impersonal Christ love."[1] Love of this kind is not "limited, selfish, personal love." God and Love were synonymous in her view. "God is Love, dear," she wrote to a personal friend. "Love is God."[2] When people truly expressed this love, it had a strong positive effect on their lives. "The love of God, expressing through the individual harmoniously, and in Christ-like ways," she wrote, "gives peace, freedom and poise."[3] She constantly emphasized the connection between the love of God and a fulfilling life. "It is the nature of divine love to give life, joy, peace, health."[4]

We connect with this power to love, Myrtle pointed out, by going within ourselves. "And where do we find love?" she asked. "Within. To be poised and balanced in the love within, is the only way to express it in one's affairs."[5] When we give out love from within, we bring harmony, and a sense of well-being, to all of our relationships. When we give love in this way, we receive it in return. "When we put aside all striving for affection," she wrote, "and give our attention to expressing love for everybody and everything, then love comes to us without seeking."[6]

Pure love involves giving rather than receiving. She told a correspondent:

> Do not think so much about receiving love as you do about expressing love. All people respond to love as a flower responds to sunshine. As sunshine brings out the colors in beauty, so the light of love brings out Christ virtues in people. So, love—love—love.[7]

It was a common pitfall to misuse divine love. "When we permit ourselves to take God's love," she wrote, "and pour it out upon a person, or things, to the degree that we bind them to ourselves, the very virtue of loving becomes a fault."[8]

Seeking love was another pitfall. "By being anxious for love, and more or less selfishly desiring that others love us," she observed, "we tend to keep love in its fullness away."[9]

> Limited personal love is always more or less a disappointment, so we must let go of the selfish element in our love if we are to realize peace of mind through love.[10]

She believed it was important to understand what was happening when we fall in love. A young woman who had fallen in love asked her advice on how to proceed. Myrtle cautioned:

> Many girls do fall in love sometimes, but they need to realize that it is an idea within *themselves* they are in love with, and not a boy or a man. So remember you are in love with an ideal, whenever you fall in love… Many folks are in love with love, and deceive themselves into believing

that it is some individual with whom they are infatuated.[11]

When we examine the nature of love in our deep love relationships we recognize that "it is really the *Divine in our loved ones* that we love so intensely."[12]

## 7. Prayer

In every letter she wrote Myrtle emphasized the need for prayer. She was convinced that through prayer people became "spiritually quickened, illumined and guided."[1] Prayer was not about asking God for favors. "Prayer is not for the purpose of petitioning God to heal you, but for the purpose of making you receptive to the good that you are asking."[2]

Myrtle devoted a great deal of time and attention to teaching her correspondents to "pray aright." No matter where or when you prayed "the idea is to get the new thought forces working positively and constantly in you."[3] She told another that prayer could "stir to action within us the vital energies that renew, strengthen and sustain mind, soul, and body."[4]

Making contact with the Christ Mind requires that you pray with regularity, preferably on a daily basis:

> Take regular times every day to go into the silence and commune with the Source of your good. It is futile to try to work things out in the outer, personally, without making contact with the Source of your help within.[5]

She contrasted the traditional Christian form of prayer with what Unity taught. Reporting on a Mother's Day address she was about to make to the Unity Young People's Forum she said:

> If I were a Catholic, I should be praying, "Hail Mother of Jesus, fill my mouth with words of wisdom and love.' As it is, I am knowing the Spirit of Motherhood, as God is implanting it in us, is prompting me, and blessing those present.[6]

Myrtle recommended prayers of praise and thanksgiving. "Through prayer and praise," she wrote, "we can all of us free ourselves from the mental prisons that bind in conditions of ignorance, sickness, sin poverty, even death."[7] It was important to give thanks, even though prayer had not produced the intended result. Myrtle advised:

> A secret of attainment is an attitude of thankfulness and rejoicing, No matter whether the good desired is manifest or still in Divine Mind,

waiting to come into expression. <u>Jesus always returned thanks to the Father before the result of his work became visible.</u>[8]

Prayer without intention to act was useless. She warned a correspondent:

> Simply to ask for prayers, and to repeat a statement of Truth, and then get up and go about your personal affairs… will not bring results. An unwise attitude will keep denying and killing out the good which prayer affirms and nurtures.[9]

Myrtle was aware that we must be careful in our asking. She told the story of a woman who prayed for the Lord to give her a husband. Myrtle reported, "Well, it took her just six weeks to "demonstrate," her man; but it took her six years of hard work, sorrow and pain to get rid of him." The lesson to be learned: "It is not always satisfactory to pray for marriage."[10]

## 8. Meditation

Words of "Truth," Myrtle maintained, were most effective and made the biggest impression on the mind if formulated in a meditative state which she referred to as "The Silence." She said:

> When you get very still and go into the silence, when you commune with your Indwelling Guide, you will be shown the easy, pleasant, harmonious and orderly way out of every situation.[1]

✳ She described the many benefits from establishing a <u>regular daily meditative practice</u>:

> The daily quiet time, for study and meditation, and identification with our Source, helps us to grow—to come into understanding of our sonship, and our full, free use of our God-given faculties and powers.[2]

Myrtle observed that people became too preoccupied with the every day mundane activities of life and failed to devote sufficient to becoming quiet and communing with God. She urged:

> We need to relax and let go and get away from ourselves. We are inclined to become so wrapped up in effects that we neglect our divine selves, and forget to draw upon the Source of life and strength.[3]

In a letter to a woman who was wondering how to go about meditating and praying, Myrtle gave special instructions:

Unity does not teach that any special physical posture is necessary. Sitting comfortably helps to bring a more restful attitude. It is the attitude of mind and heart, our interest and earnestness, that helps you most to the "Still Place" within. Follow the instructions given in Matthew 6:6. The "closet" is your heart center. Do not make a difficulty of entering the silence. Remember that the silence is prayer; and as you consecrate your thinking and living to God, your whole life becomes a prayer. It is very easy to close our eyes and think deep down into the stillness within ourselves, and get God's message through our own minds.[4]

Failure to pay proper attention to the inner life has its consequences. She warned, "When we spend so much time working on the outer without setting aside needed periods to gather new strength in the silence, we get the results of our sewing."[5]

One of the best ways to manifest the Christ Consciousness was during silent meditation:

When we are in the silence we become open and receptive to the inflow of the holy spirit, which fills every part of us, and makes us new and strong and whole.[6] … As you still all the outer thoughts and meditate on the Indwelling Christ, you will be spiritually quickened uplifted and strengthened. You will be inspired with new and rich ideas and will demonstrate good things for you.[7]

Myrtle recognized that many people considered meditation to be a waste of time. For those who doubted its value she suggested:

Instead of striving in a intense outer and personal way to demonstrate your sufficiency, go into the silence and declare the Word; then rest in the faith that the power of the Word is working to bring forth the wisdom, health, strength and supply you need… This inner way is the only way to bring into manifestation, here and now, the inheritance that is yours by Divine Right.[8]

## 9. Focusing on the present moment

It is not surprising that someone who spent time meditating each day would see value in keeping the mind focused on the present moment. "Here and now is the place of more abundant life, and the real Christ joy."[1] … Live life itself one moment at a time."[2]

She urged her correspondents to stay present. "Live in the present," she urged, "live in the Now, treat every moment like a new beginning… get a firm hold on the idea that it is what we are Now that really counts."[3]

It was fruitless to focus on what was going to happen in the future. Hence, she advised a correspondent:

> **Instead of looking off into the future that is six months away, or six weeks away, or six minutes off, know and rejoice that God, Omnipresent Good and wisdom, is meeting your every need this moment, and will continue to do so throughout eternity.**[4]

Allowing the mind to dwell on the past is equally counterproductive. You will defeat yourself, she explained, "if you let old fears, personal feelings and negative beliefs of the previous moment bridge the interval of time and feed upon the substance of the present moment."[5] It is essential "to protect your mind substance, that of the present moment, this very moment, this very second, from being sullied by any averse thoughts of the previous moment."[6]

Myrtle was passionate about the need to stay focused on the here and now, as she told a correspondent:

> **Right now you have fresh substance, fresh in this new moment of your existence, and the God-given power to use it to absolutely renew, regenerate and spiritualize your mind, body, and affairs.[7] We must live in the now and let your new thoughts be nourished by this spiritual bread… Grasp the freshness and newness of this present second, with its new thoughts and inspirations.**[8]

## 10. Joy

"Joy is one of our powerful spiritual assets," Myrtle asserted. "Joy relieves all strain and stress and opens the way for the outpouring of divine goodness."[1] She indicated how joy worked to heighten consciousness:

> **Joy is light. Joy sends its shining beams through out the consciousness. It dissipates all discouraged, doubted states of mind, all fear and apprehension. It lifts one on the wings of the morning to the spiritual heights where all the things are seen in their right relation.**[2]

Myrtle indicated that our health improved when we were joyous:

When you tune your consciousness to the note of joy and harmony, you body temple will respond wonderfully, and you will experience the freedom, lightness and health that you long to express.[3]

Myrtle suggested an affirmation which she indicated would increase a person's ability to experience the joy of living:

Start with the top of your head and go to the very bottom of your feet, into every organ, every function, every nerve, every cell in your body temple, giving each the word of joy. Do not simply speak the word of joy to them but make this word ringing, sparkling, living and vibrant… Use it every day and many times a day both silently and aloud until your whole being is actively vibrantly awake and alive with the joy of living.[4]

## 11. Spiritual messages in dreams

Myrtle indicated that she had received valuable spiritual messages in dreams. She believed that dreams, if properly interpreted, provided spiritual guidance. They revealed "the character of our thinking."[1] Their meaning could be derived if we understood their symbolic nature. "Dreams are clothed in symbols, and when we interpret them aright, we have a key to the lessons that come to us."[2]

Dreams had played an important role in her own life. She had a powerful dream about the nature of the divine while a student studying geology, and making excursions into the country to study rock formations and waterfalls. Only after years had passed was she able to interpret the message contained in the dream. This is the dream, as she related it:

One night in my dreams I took a wonderful trip all by myself, and this is what I found—the bed of a stream that must have been active at some time. It was beautiful, with a white sandy bottom, but all the water it held was in a few bowls of white rock—apparently a dried up stream. Stopping to investigate, I could found no source. A very high ledger of rock crossed its bed at the south, and looking to the north I could see only a continuous bed of like character as that before me. In my astonishment I voiced the question "From whence is the source of this stream?" And for the answer came a sudden voice, more of waters than anything else, "I will show you," and over the ledge of rock came pouring a regular Niagara. I had to get back in the woods away from the spray. It ceased when the bed was filled. As I stood looking at the clear waters of the stream, beautiful flowers sprang up.[3]

The meaning of the dream came to her at a time when she was very ill. She reported:

> When my life stream was so low and I was about to lose it, there came pouring forth this truth. I saw more clearly the meaning of this dream. I remembered where the source of my life was and how it came over the rock that was higher than I.[4]

Two other lengthy dreams that provided Myrtle with important spiritual information can be found in Appendix Two.

Myrtle advised her correspondents to work with their dreams. She offered assistance in getting at the deeper meaning of dreams, and as a result, many people sent dreams to her for interpretation. Even though letter-writing left something to be desired as a format for interpreting dreams, Myrtle did her best, even though her correspondents probably didn't always provide sufficient information for Myrtle to provide clues to their meaning. Her responses contained words of encouragement, and she always left her correspondents with the feeling that they were on the right track when they paid attention to dreams.

## 12. Persistence

Persistence and determination were needed to overcome the constraints of the carnal mind and manifest the Christ Consciousness. Myrtle elaborated:

> We don't usually accomplish many things worthwhile, without steadfastness and persistent effort, as well as prayerful contemplation of all the factors involved.[1]

Constant effort is required to root out the negativity that invades our minds:

> It takes fearlessness and courage and persistence to unseat the assertions of adverse belief. But fearlessness and courage and persistence and love can unseat all assumptions of that which is contrary to the out work of infinite good.[2]

Myrtle indicated that "we must grow, work, and think out things for ourselves."[3] The Christ-life would not be handed to us:

> You will have to want it enough to actually make the effort to do it … The Spirit of God in you is willing, but you must demand of the flesh

that it obey the spirit."[4]

If we were not required to put for the necessary effort, she noted:

> We should be more like pigs than men. We would simply wallow around, and take the good things handed out and eat them, and go to sleep—and grunt if we were disturbed.[5]

## 13. Faith

Central to Myrtle's spiritual teaching was the belief that the divine lay within. "Put your faith," she said, "in your own indwelling Lord."[1] Truth Principles are based on faith in the spiritual power of the Christ Consciousness, "To do anything," she said, "it is necessary to have faith.[2] . . . Your faith is the "button" that turns on the inner light and quickens it."[3]

Good things happen when you truly believe, as she told a correspondent. When you put your faith "in your innate Christ wholeness and perfection, you are bound to overcome all the wrong conditions that have limited you.[4]

Doubt and faith cannot co-exist, and Myrtle had this advice for those whose faith wavered:

> When doubts come into your mind, it is your job to put them out and keep them out. You can fill your mind so full of faith in God that there will not be room for doubt to even open the door.[5]

Faith required that you be singled-minded, as she told a correspondent:

> Don't be like the woman who prayed one night that the mountain near her house be removed, and then the next morning went to the window to see if it was still there, and when she saw it was still there she said, "I knew it would be." If we keep our eye on the condition and one eye on God, we are building two kinds of structures. We are commanded to keep our eyes "single to the Good."[6]

Myrtle indicated that faith could be strengthen through spiritual practice:

> Your faith and belief are not things that come from outside yourself. They are Divine attributes that were implanted in your soul from the beginning, and what you need to do is to awaken them, strengthen and develop them through prayer, spiritual meditation, and by keeping your mind filled with the faith idea.[7]

Myrtle indicated how faith could be put to use most effectively:

> There is nothing like the exercise of the spiritual faith which sees prayer already answered to bring results quickly. "Before they call, I will answer; and while they are speaking, I will hear." When you pray, believe whole-heartedly that this glorious promise is fulfilled unto you.[8]

## Divine Law

Truth principles, Myrtle indicated, operated in accordance with Divine Law. "Truth principles are laws," she said. When men and women understood and followed these laws, their lives worked well on all levels, physically, psychologically and spiritually.[1]

When Myrtle felt one of her correspondents was manifesting the Christ Mind she might say, as she told a correspondent "You are meeting life from the basis of divine law."[2] Divine law, or "spiritual laws" as she also referred to them, took many forms. She referred to them as:

> The law of your being; The law of giving and receiving; The Law of Good; The law of life; The law of God; The law of progress; The law of thought; The Prosperity law; and the three-fold law of life and health and harmony.[3]

In letters to correspondents, in which she recommended one of these divine laws, she never fully explained how the particular law worked, or how specifically to live within it. This lack of clarity must have confused many correspondents.

## The Twelve Powers

"The Twelve Powers" are the words Charles and Myrtle Fillmore used to describe the human attributes that men and women needed to develop in order to manifest the Christ within. They also called them the "faculties of the mind." Charles Fillmore listed the Twelve in his book *The Twelve Powers of Man*:

1. Faith
2. Strength
3. Discrimination or Judgment
4. Love.
5. Power
6. Imagination

7. Understanding
8. Will.
9. Order
10. Zeal
11. Renunciation
12. Life Conserver

Information on the doctrine appeared early in their teaching, as articles on the Twelve Powers first appeared in *Thought and Unity* magazines in the 1890s. Articles in *Unity* describing one, sometimes two or three, of the Twelve Powers appeared occasionally thereafter. However, the doctrine was not presented fully in book form until 1930 when Charles published *The Twelve Powers of Man*.

Since Myrtle's letters from 1928 to 1931 occasionally mentioned the Powers, it is likely that she wrote about them many times in her forty years of counseling correspondents. She probably began telling her correspondents about the Twelve Powers when she and Charles began developing them in the 1890s.

The following letter to a correspondent contains one of her more complete descriptions of them. She wrote:

> We have found that there are twelve central or basic centers of consciousness, which are the result of the soul's use of the God qualities of Life and Love, and Wisdom and Power and Substance. These centers of consciousness are mental, but they have built the physical organism through which they express. So, we have twelve locations in the body, where the soul expresses divine qualities, which to make up the Christ consciousness—at least we term it Christ consciousness when the individual is expressing himself under divine law. Understanding is located in the throat; but this is the positive pole of the quality, and it is through the exercise of this faculty that man expresses his spiritual understanding and makes use of the unseen and mental realm. Faith and understanding will lead you forth into the discovery and use of all the other faculties, and you will become in fact the rounded expression of the Christ which you are initially.[1]

In many of her letters Myrtle did not provide enough information for a correspondent to gain an understanding of how the Twelve Powers functioned. For example, in the following letter Myrtle describes the benefits activating each of the powers, but provides little guidance on how to work with them:

Right use of wisdom will prompt you in doing that which will result in success. Right use of power will give mastery and poise and the ability to work well with your fellows. Right use of life will keep your whole system built up, and a good healthy satisfied feeling in every part. Right use of love will make you kind and considerate and diligent in doing what is best for all of your dear ones, and also keep your mental faculties and your members and the various functions of your body doing that what is best for each other, so harmony will prevail, and there will be no craving for harmful stimulants. Right use of substance will build you up, and provide well for your family, and give you something to keep you really interested in your progress.[2]

In another letter she indicates that all the powers need to be developed, but never tells her correspondent how to proceed:

All the divine powers must be called forth, as Jesus called the twelve disciples. The Christ man needs all of his faculties—power and strength, wisdom and love, order, praise, zeal imagination, faith, judgment, understanding, elimination—organized and unified in constructive activity.[3]

She chastises another correspondent for failing to discipline her mind. She then lists the powers, but doesn't tell her correspondent how to activate them:

Your mind has wandered into the abstract, in thinking about God, and heaven and spiritual ministry, until you have been unable to direct the work of faith, and love and power and life, and wisdom, and zeal and order, and judgment and will and renunciation, and imagination and strength through the centers formed in your body for the expression of these God qualities that He has implanted in you.[4]

In another letter Myrtle provides an affirmation which might be used to activate the Twelve Powers, but provides no context, or description of the faculties themselves:

The Christ Mind is now quickening all my faculties. Looking away from appearances I intuitively perceive all things in their right relationships. All my powers and all my senses are refined and given righteous expression, and I see but one path before me, and I walk fearlessly and joyously into it. All my decisions are wise.[5]

Myrtle was disappointed that many of her correspondents failed to grasp her teaching. It must have been a source of frustration that she was not always able to get her message across. She told a correspondent:

> We know from our own experience, and from many, many letters which come from people everywhere, that there is almost universal lack of understanding of the Truth of Being.[6]

## *Bodily Regeneration*

Like Charles, Myrtle believed that if men and women fully manifested the Christ within that they would regenerate the cells of their bodies, remain eternally youthful and overcome physical death. She told a correspondent:

> The sooner we purify and spiritualize the organism, the sooner will we be free from the carnal law.[1] ... When we learn how to find the Christ in ourselves, and draw constantly upon the inner fountain of life, our youth will be renewed as the days and years go by. Time will but increase our strength and youthfulness, because we will be under the law of Spirit, instead of under the law of sin and the "last enemy." [death][2]

Myrtle said that the doctrine came to them during periods of meditation:

> My experience has been that Mr. Fillmore and I have been a great help to each other. As we prayed and meditated together in the silence holding the same prayers, the law of regeneration gradually unfolded to us.[3]

Like Charles, Myrtle believed that Jesus set the example by overcoming physical death and regenerating his body:

> Jesus Christ raised the body consciousness, through His realization of the Absolute, and identified it with the spiritual body, the character of which is so transcendent as to be beyond human concept. This is the body in which Jesus now lives, and in which we shall all enter when we have lifted up the body idea, and set free the forces that enter into it. Paul said, "Christ in you, Hope of Glory," and the coming forth of the life of Christ in every man is Regeneration, which Unity stresses in its teachings.[4]

Myrtle acknowledged that to her knowledge Jesus was the only one that had accomplished this feat. Nevertheless, she believed that if Jesus could do it, we could also:

> As far as we know Jesus is the only one who has overcome "the last enemy" [death] but those who follow him in the regeneration can overcome as He did if they are diligent and faithful.[5]

Myrtle was under no illusions as to how many humans then alive would commit themselves to follow the path of regeneration. She lamented the fact that many people were not spiritually ready for it:

> We do not condemn generation. It is all right for those who are not highly evolved… Thousands of children are born to those who are not yet ready for regeneration.[6]

When asked what progress she and Charles had made in regenerating their bodies, she replied:

> You asked if Mr. Fillmore or I have put on the new body yet. We are on the way, and are finding that our bodies are being refined, renewed and spiritualized continually. Even the new body must become finer purer, more spiritual, for it must keep up with the conscious mind in the renewing process. There is no standing still. All of us must continually go forward and upward.[7]

The information Myrtle provided to her correspondents on bodily regeneration was often incomplete and probably confusing. It is unlikely that her correspondents understood the teaching. For example, in the following letter to correspondent she described her commitment to bodily regeneration, but provided little or no information on how to proceed:

> Unity teaches the regeneration taught and demonstrated by Christ Jesus, and all who aspire to eternal health and prosperity, and even eternal life here and now, are accepting the way of regeneration.[8]

Given her strong commitment to the practice, it is surprising that most of her letters to correspondents, written between 1928 and 1931, did not mention regeneration. When she did recommend it, the information she provided was sketchy.

Myrtle gave more information in this letter on the benefits of regeneration, but probably not enough to inspire her correspondent to begin the process:

We have consecrated our whole lives to the Jesus Christ teaching, and we believe that those who are steadfast in practicing its principles that he demonstrated will overcome the death of the body, just as he did. One on the essentials in attaining of eternal life and the redemption of the body, is to keep the attention undivided and fixed upon the *Life of God Within.*[9]

## Reincarnation

Myrtle believed that the physical death of the body did not extinguish the life of the spirit. Contrary to the traditional Christian belief that the soul had one opportunity to achieve everlasting life with Jesus in heaven, Myrtle believed that it took many lifetimes for a soul to complete its spiritual work. She wrote:

Every one of us is going to have to reincarnate until we make the union of Spirit, soul, and body, and spiritualize these bodies of ours.[1]

She consoled another correspondent, saying, "Know that this soul will get the lessons needed, and that the divine law of life will give just the right opportunity for further expression and growth."[2]

Myrtle described what she believed life was like after physical death:

The soul continues just as it is, except that it no longer has the vehicle of expression. The thing called death is more like sleep than living. It is a sort of rest—like our night's sleep and rest.[3]

In another letter she told a correspondent that a loved one would return for more spiritual work:

When the time comes the way will open so that that she can through reincarnation again take up a vehicle of flesh, and come into the world to do the will of I AM, her own indwelling Lord.[4]

Myrtle did not believe that anyone went to hell, the place that many traditional Christians believed that souls were required to go because of having lived a sinful life: She wrote

Our preachers have sought to frighten their people into being good by describing this state of torment and burning as a condition which they would face after death.[5]

Myrtle felt this teaching discouraged men and women from focusing on their spirituality: "Those who have learned this version of "Hell" are sometimes less spiritually minded than they might be."[6]

## Influences

Myrtle Fillmore, along with her husband Charles, read widely in the spiritual literature of their day. Their spiritual periodical, *Modern Thought* magazine, first published in April 1889, contained articles from a variety of spiritual teachings, philosophical schools and religious outlooks. These included the scriptural teachings of Jesus, the Transcendentalist works of Ralph Waldo Emerson, the Christian metaphysics of Warren Felt Evans, the Theosophical works of Helen Petrovna Blavatsky, the Christian Science of Mary Baker Eddy, and several who reinterpreted Eddy's work, including Emma Curtis Hopkins.

The Fillmores were also acquainted with Hermetic Philosophy, Spiritualism. the religions of the East—Buddhism and Hindism, as well as the works of Emanuel Swedenborg. It is a mystery as to how they accomplished this by the spring of 1889 when they began *Modern Thought* magazine. Myrtle was forty-four at the time, the mother of two young sons, and a former Clinton, Missouri school teacher. Charles was a thirty-five-year-old Kansas City businessman with no formal education. It is apparent that Myrtle and Charles were two extremely bright, curious and spiritually engaged people, who spent a great deal of time acquainting themselves with a wide range of spiritual literature.

The three spiritual teachers the Fillmores appeared to rely upon the most in developing the Unity teaching were Ralph Waldo Emerson, Warren Felt Evans, and Emma Curtis Hopkins.

Charles expressed their indebtedness to Ralph Waldo Emerson:

> **All students of metaphysics should read Emerson. His writings contain the essence of all the higher thoughts that are now being so lavishly given the world through Christian Science, Metaphysics, Theosophy, and the various systems of soul culture.**[1] **... Emerson anticipates and gave voice in his essays to all the truths which have formulated into divine science. His writings are growing more popular daily and no metaphysical student should be without this volume of his works.**[2]

Warren Felt Evans (1817–1889) was the first American writer to give literary form to the ideas and methods of spiritual healing. His book *Mental Healing*, published in 1869, was widely read in the United States and Europe, went through several editions and was published in several languages. Charles read Evans' works—he wrote seven books—and there is every reason to believe Myrtle did too. In 1908 Charles commented:

> W.E. Evans is called "The Recording Angel of Metaphysics." He has hunted out the vital issues in ancient and modern spiritual writing, and sifted them thoroughly. I have read the seven volumes which he has written and think them the most complete of all metaphysical compilations.[3]

Emma Curtis Hopkins, author of *High Mysticism*, had been a student of Mary Baker Eddy, but had broken away from Eddy and was teaching her own brand of Christian Science when she came to Kansas City in 1890 to teach a series of classes. The Fillmores attended and came away singing her praises. Charles wrote, "Certain persons have the faculty of imparting knowledge of this great principle more readily than others, and Mrs. Hopkins is one in whom this faculty is especially developed."[4] Myrtle was also high in her praise, stating "I know of no other writings which mean so much to me as hers do."[5]

# ❧ 3 ❧
## *Practitioner of Spiritual Healing*

hile Myrtle was firmly committed to knowing and understanding the principles of the "Truth of Being" and teaching them to others, she had an equally strong commitment to putting Truth principles into practice. Myrtle indicated that, at age forty-two in 1887, the tuberculosis that she had contracted as a young woman, and from which she almost died, was no longer a factor in her life. She attributed her healing to practicing Truth Principles. She told a correspondent:

> You ask what restored me to vigorous health. It was a change of mind from the old, carnal mind that believes in sickness to the Christ Mind of life and permanent health. "Be ye transformed by the renewal of your mind" (Rom. 12:2). "As he thinketh in his heart, so is he" (Prov. 23:7A.V). I applied spiritual laws effectively, blessing my body temple until it manifested the innate health of spirit.[1]

She soon began using the same principles in seeking to remedy the physical ailments of others. Her first efforts were in her own home with her laundress who was suffering from bronchitis. Myrtle recalled:

> My attention was attracted to her continual coughing. Upon inquiry I found that she had bronchitis; a little cold had given it an active form, and she was spitting blood. It occurred to me that here was an opportunity to apply my divine remedy, and I said, "Lucy, I have found a new way to gain health, and I am going to try it on you." I turned within myself, and for the first time gave what might be called a "Treatment". Imagine my joy when I found that the effect was instantaneous. I interviewed her three weeks after, and she informed me that she had never coughed from the time of that treatment. After that she always looked to me to remedy her physical ailments.[2]

She then worked with her own children who had often been sick. She told how she proceeded:

> I had always been a very anxious, solicitous mother to our two sons, the younger of whom was a mere baby. The elder was subject to tonsillitis. The tonsils were becoming chronically enlarged, and the doctors said that nothing but the removal of them would meet the

requirements of the case… Our younger boy had a tendency toward the croup. There are few mothers who do not understand the terror of being awakened in the night by the hoarse signal that portends this dreaded ailment of childhood… With my new understanding, I started to teach my little ones that there is nothing in all God's world to fear.[3]

Friends and neighbors soon observed her ability to heal and sought her help. "Others saw that there was something new in me," she recalled. "And they asked me to share it. I did."[4] Her eldest son, Lowell, who was still a young boy when Myrtle began giving treatments, remembered an old Irishman, who worked as a delivery man, and came to the house for help with his legs. Lowell reported:

I think for many years his legs had been stiff with rheumatism and he had to go on crutches. He would come to the house. I was a boy then. Mother would tell him to get up and walk. He would laugh and try to walk, though his knees were weak and creaked a good deal. But he would walk; in three treatments he was pretty well, and soon he was absolutely healed. I saw him a number of years later… He had grown up and he was hopping in and out of an express wagon.[5]

In letters to correspondents Myrtle described some of the people she had treated and the results that had been attained. She recalled a case in which she responded to a call from a woman who, she said had been "given up by the medical profession." When Myrtle arrived at the woman's home she noticed shelves containing row after row of bottles of medicine. "I just filled those bottles with the elixir of life," Myrtle remembered. "I spoke the word for the patient, and trustfully enfolded all in His loving power. The result was an instant healing."[6]

Myrtle described how she was called to the house of a woman who had an obstruction in her throat. The woman reported a "smothering sensation" that hampered her breathing. Myrtle reported, "She would cough, without apparent relief. There would be times when it seemed she would pass out." Myrtle said that she talked with the woman and prayed for her. Then she went home. A little later the woman's daughter telephoned Myrtle and exclaimed, "You can't guess what has happened to Mother! Why, she was seized with violent coughing, and coughed up a pea—firm and round and fresh looking. And now she's all right, and relieved of the coughing." Myrtle explained how, in her view, prayer had worked. "The new energy and spiritual assurance which resulted from the treatment gave her more strength and power, to dislodge the pea. God knows how to work and to relieve us and to heal us, when our faith is centered within, and when we decide to accept and make use of His help."[7]

Myrtle also described a case in which a medical doctor testified that her treatment work had effected a surprising cure. In this case, Myrtle's female client had undergone an operation to have the walls of her vagina sewn up. Within a short time the woman was told by the doctor that the walls had broken down again and that another operation was necessary. At this point, Myrtle said, "She came to us for treatment." Myrtle reported that while working with her client, "she gained a knowledge of Truth" and was healed. Returning to her doctor for a checkup the physician was astounded to find that the walls of her vagina had been almost entirely rebuilt. "What have you been doing?" the doctor asked. Myrtle's client told about the treatment work she received at Unity. The doctor responded, "You had better keep on with people who can do that."[8]

A friend and Kansas City neighbor, Pearl Duval, reported a healing that took place in her family shortly after Myrtle began seeing clients. A relative of Mrs. Duval's, a woman from a small town outside Kansas City, had brought her six-year-old son, Robert Waller, who was crippled and couldn't walk into Kansas City for medical attention. Doctors told the family that nothing could be done for the boy and that he would be crippled for life. Mrs. Duval recalled how Myrtle became involved:

> At the time Mr. and Mrs. Fillmore lived in the same block where the boy was staying. The children all played together and this little boy had heard of "that lady that heals," and he said, "I want to see that lady that heals." One day while playing he went alone up to the house. Mrs. Fillmore came to the door, took him in her arms, talked with him, raising the child in consciousness to the healing presence of the Christ within him. She prayed, believed, and the child walked home.[9]

Mrs. Duval concluded the story by stating that Robert Waller was now a grown man fifty years old, "has four fine children, and has never been on crutches from that day to this."

Tesla Wallace Landon, whose mother and father were friends of the Fillmores and involved with Unity work, almost from the beginning, testified that her parents called Myrtle to their home for prayer work when her younger brother was born in 1903. Landon described Myrtle's participation:

I had a baby brother born in 1903. Myrtle Fillmore was in our home at that time. The only way the Doctor would take the case was with the understanding that Myrtle stand by. Everything came through beautifully. He was named Theodore Fillmore Wallace.[10]

As Myrtle's treatment work grew she discovered that she was successful even with very difficult cases. She knew it was wrong to take credit personally, and was quick to acknowledge that it was not she, herself, but the divine working through her, that did the healing:

The Lord worked so easily and so freely that I think that those who came all went away feeling well. There were cases that were considered hopeless; yet although the doctors had given them up, the Lord healed them. A child who was blind was healed. That showed what the Lord could do, and I was very happy.[11]

Myrtle was convinced that the key to her success was faith in the healing power of the God within:

I will say that in those early days I hardly knew just what was taking place as the healings were accomplished. I only knew that my experience was much like that of the blind man whom Jesus healed; "One thing I know, that whereas I was blind, now I see." I simply put great faith that God, the loving Father, had marvelously revealed himself to me as my help in every need, and my faith inspired others to have faith.[12]

When she began her healing work Myrtle was primarily concerned with enabling people to overcome their physical and psychological maladies and return to good health. She soon came to realize that physical healing was only one aspect of the work. The real goal was advancing the spiritual development of the patient. Myrtle described her attitude toward healing when she first began practicing, and how her viewpoint evolved:

At that time healing seemed the most important thing in life to me. I loved seeing folks get well and happy. I do yet, but I have learned that the spiritual awakening and the daily development of Christ powers are more important. The soul must be awakened and brought to a realization of the Truth, and encouraged in the righteous use of all the God-given faculties and powers. The individual must be helped to

**unify his spirit, soul, and body in harmonious spiritual living here and now.**[13]

Charles joined Myrtle as a practitioner of spiritual healing sometime in the early 1890s. A large part of their work day was devoted to treating clients who came to their offices. Outside their offices in the Hall building in Kansas City hung a sign in bold letters with the words "Mental Healing." The sign listed both Myrtle and Charles as "Teachers and Healers. Office hours were posted as "10–4" daily.[14] *Unity* magazine also published a "Teachers and Healers" directory in which the services of Charles and Myrtle were listed.

In 1896 Charles gave an indication of the size of their client load when he observed that during the workday at their offices, "a continuous stream of people go and come."[15] It appears that a significant part of the income needed to support their family during the first two decades of their work came from clients who came to see them for treatment work. Both appeared to have a large number of clients. Myrtle testified that she "saw the hearts of people as they really are. People would come out day after day and take treatments."[16] Charles also proved to be an effective healer. Lowell recalled, "I can remember how the reception room would be lined with people. He had some wonderful cures, and these had as much to do with the success of the work as anything."[17]

In 1909, when Charles gave up practitioner work, he estimated that during the preceding twenty years he had treated on the average twenty clients each day.[18] We have no testimony about the size of Myrtle's clientele, but given the success she had, and the fact that by the late 1890s she began training people to help with the healing work in the Unity offices, it is probable that her load was equal to or greater than her husband's.

Charging people for healing work seemed wrong to Myrtle. At the outset of her work in the mid-1880s. Myrtle said that she never thought about payment. "We saw that our ministry was God's ministry and beyond money values—that it was a ministry in values that could not be paid for in commercial ways, only in gratitude, love and living the Truth."[19] Charles at the time was doing well in business in Kansas City and the family, according to Myrtle, didn't need the money. "I didn't think about compensation," she reported. "The joy of seeing people well and happy was compensation enough for me."

Nevertheless people wanted to compensate her for her efforts, and she was uncertain whether it was appropriate to take money or accept gifts. "I was perfectly astonished," she recalled, "to see that everybody wanted to do something for me… At first I wondered whether it was right for me to take gifts." She ultimately decided to accept them, she said, "because they were given with such joy and gladness." Later, as she reflected upon the issue of compensation, she concluded that it was right that she should be remunerated for her services. She observed that there was a spiritual law which said, "when you give your best you get the best… I saw that many other people had to understand that they too must give their best."[20]

Nonetheless she felt it wrong to set a price for her services. "I said to my husband, 'We are doing God's work; how can we charge for something that God is giving to people'?" They resolved the question by devising the free-will offering plan, a method by which people were provided with the opportunity to give for services received without being charged a specific amount. A basket for contributions was left in their waiting room. Myrtle convinced herself of the importance of accepting payment with this logic: "If God gives us something to give and the first step in healing needs to be that people be willing to give as well as to receive, then my part is to be as willing to receive as I am to give."[21]

As their workload increased, and as the men and women who studied with them became qualified to teach and heal, the Fillmores invited others to practice spiritual healing with them in their Kansas City offices. In the late 1890s Cassius Shafer, a local Kansas City man, who later began a Unity center in Chicago, was the first healer to join them in the offices at 1315 McGee Street.[22] By 1909, after moving to larger quarters on Tracy street, four healers, including Myrtle, were in attendance at Unity headquarters. *Weekly Unity* announced their availability:

> **On the second floor of the Unity building, 913 Tracy Avenue, are our local healing rooms where city clients are treated. Mrs. Myrtle Fillmore, Mrs. A.H. Ray, Mrs. Sophia Van Marter and Mrs. Rudesill have charge of this ministry and will be in attendance daily at certain hours.**[23]

Unity further stated that local healers "look after patients who desire the personality of the practitioner to appear before them. Potential clients were assured that they would be "served with careful attention."[24] Those whom the Fillmores chose to work with them were required to meet specific standards. Myrtle described the qualifications a healer must possess. She stated:

Those who meet the public are supposed to be poised and well rounded in spiritual development, and so filled with love and joy and health and consciousness of supply that they fairly radiate it to all who come near—not starved for kindness and understanding and love and encouragement. Those who need help themselves don't belong in the work where they are continually faced with the problems of others... So long as you are so disturbed by what others do or fail to do, you are hardly abiding in the Christ consciousness, from which you should work in spiritual ministry.[25]

The number of local healers never grew beyond a half dozen during the remaining two decades of Myrtle Fillmore's life. Today, at Unity Church Universal, located at 913 Tracy in Kansas City, in the building constructed in 1906 to house Unity headquarters, the visitor can see the room on the third floor where Myrtle had her office, and the rooms where the other local healers worked.

Myrtle Fillmore devoted less time to practitioner work as years passed, though she never totally gave it up. Ila White, a woman who served for a time as her secretary, reported as late as 1929, just two years before Myrtle died, that she spent one day each week in healing work. White said that, "The work of the local Unity society needs Mrs. Fillmore's wonderful mother-love and care, and she devotes Wednesdays to it."[26]

# 4
## Silent Unity

Absent healing, as the Silent Unity work is called, was begun by Myrtle and Charles in the late 1880s. It was called absent healing because the healer was not physically present with the client when the work took place. Myrtle described the philosophy which supported the work in an article entitled "Absent Healing," which appeared in the inaugural issue of *Modern Thought* magazine in 1890. It was at the beginning of her work as a practitioner of spiritual healing and as a teacher of Truth Principles. She wrote:

> There is therefore a great and present reality and a profound philosophy in the doctrine and practice designated as "absent treatment." It is not imaginary… The philosophy is well supported by facts, by excellent evidence and testimonies from all quarters… I have seen very manifest effects from it, perhaps as clear and striking as those that flow from present treatment. Therefore, this absent treatment, so called is one of the noblest and most beautiful phenomena that can be contemplated. It was always deemed sacred to pray for the absent… It is an intelligent and philosophical laying hold of eternal life for the benefit of others.[1]

Myrtle finished the article with a prediction, "May this this power be mightily developed. It is destined to become an unspeakable blessing to mankind."

In the 1890s the Fillmores provided absent healing through an organization called the Society for Silent Unity. In 1891 *Unity* magazine was founded to provide spiritual advice and counsel to people who enrolled as members of the Society.[2] One of the main goals of the Society was to reach out to those who were unable to have "the benefit of personal healing or teaching.[3] Members of the society were encouraged to develop themselves spiritually by studying Truth principles, by practicing meditation and engaging in the practice of spiritual healing. Through articles in *Unity* the Fillmores taught Truth principles to members of the Society. Special columns presented "such points of Truth as are suitable for beginners."[4]

Membership in the society was open to "every soul in the Universe."[5] Members were asked to sit in the silence at 9 p.m. each evening and to hold in mind an affirmation entitled the "Class Thought." Class thoughts, which were published monthly in *Unity* magazine, were for the purpose of connecting the member with the spirit of God within, as the following examples indicate:

**"I am now manifesting the perfect harmony of Omnipotent Mind."[6]**

**"I am now conscious of thy Indwelling Presence."[7]**

Myrtle and Charles, through editorial notes in *Unity*, indicated that they were willing to provide absent healing should members choose to write for help. Their approach was low-key. They did not actively encourage members to write to them. They warned members that, because of their busy schedules, they could not always answer their letters personally, but that they would "respond in silence as Spirit directs."[8]

By 1893 the Fillmores were getting more letter requests for absent healing than they could handle personally. A woman who identified herself as "Secretary McMahon" was apparently the first person they trained to handle these requests. She was probably the first healer—they were later to be called prayer workers—for what was now being called "The Silent Unity Healing Department."

Secretary McMahon wrote an article for *Unity* magazine in 1893 in which she commented on the cases being treated, not only by herself, but by other members of the department. She described her work as a letter writer and spiritual healer. She cited the cases of several people whose physical ills had been alleviated through absent healing.[9] The work of the Silent Unity Healing Department proceeded slowly in the 1890s, as there was no effort to promote the work. The primary goal was to respond to requests from members of the Society for Silent Unity.

By 1901, the Silent Unity Healing Department had, in addition to the Fillmores, three others who were engaged in absent healing at Unity headquarters—Mr. and Mrs. Cassius Shafer and Jennie Croft. In *Unity* magazine in January 1901, the Fillmores assured Society of Silent Unity members that the healers at Unity headquarters welcomed their requests for spiritual work, and indicated that valuable help would be provided:

> **We are ready to help you all to come into the Christ Presence and Power. The power is mighty in us, and we are assured that we can help others to realize it… As a Spiritual Center we send forth the Christ Word for all members and for the friends of members. There is no limit to the power of the Divine Logos where there is a faith center in working order. If you have faith that God can reach your friends in their trials, mental or physical, send forth your spiritual word and God**

will provide it for you. If you have faith in Silent Unity, write or wire us, and our power will be joined with yours.[10]

In early 1905, the Fillmores began on a regular basis to encourage subscribers of *Unity* magazine, in addition to those who were members of the Society for Silent Unity, to write to them for spiritual counseling and healing. They used full page ads in *Unity* encourage people to get in touch with them:

We can help you in matters pertaining to health, finances, spiritual understanding, and in fact, everything that is desirable, and for your highest good… We put no limit on the power of the Holy Spirit, through which the work is done. Write us freely just what you most desire.[11]

By 1907 the Fillmores had become convinced—based on the testimony of those that had been treated in absentia—that absent healing was even more effective than the practitioner work they had been engaged in for years with clients in Kansas City:

Some folks think they will get better results if they are treated by an individual healer, but our experience is that the healing averages higher where cases are handled from an impersonal standpoint. There is good reason for this—the work is not done by the healer, but by the Spirit of Truth, and where both patient and helper forget self and center all power in the Great Supreme, the consciousness is raised to a higher plane and the result Divine.[12]

While no statistics are available prior to 1907, on the number of letters and telegrams received or sent, the number of healers working at Unity headquarters in Kansas City rose, in the six years between 1900 and 1906, from three to eleven.[13] In order to make to make it easier, both for those who wanted "healing and spiritual assistance," and those responding to them in the Silent Unity Healing Department, the Fillmores urged: "Write short letters. A little silent prayer before you write… will help you tell us your needs clearly and concisely."[14]

In January 1907 *Unity* reported on the Silent Unity Healing Department's workload, stating that about one hundred letters were being written daily. The magazine also published extracts from letters "written by Silent Unity healers to patients." These extracts, the Fillmores indicated, provided "excellent lessons," therefore were "worthy of repeating to all of our readers."[15] These letters were viewed as presenting the teaching in direct and accessible form.

Periodically, further details about the workings of the Silent Unity Healing Department were presented in *Unity*. In August 1908 the following report reflected its growing importance:

> **The absent healing and correspondence department of our work is seldom mentioned in these columns but it is none the less important. A dozen people give their entire efforts to this part of the work, and have set apart a large room in the Unity building where no one enters but those who are dedicated to the ministry. Here the power of the Omnipresent One is realized until its presence fills the room and goes forth with every word that is there—thought, written, or spoken. The correspondence of this Silent Unity Department is strictly private, but many letters testify to the healing, spiritualizing and comforting effects of the ministry.[16]**

With a growing staff of full-time healers working at Unity headquarters, it could not be expected that people doing this work would not be compensated for their services. The Fillmores took the position that they would not charge a fee for absent healing, and that it needed to be done on a freewill offering basis.[17] They considered it improper to charge for spiritual work. "Our work is not to be bought for a price. We make no bargain or ask any pay."[18] Free will offerings, they observed, were a well-established practice in religious circles in America. "The religious institutions of this country depend upon freewill offerings of the people for their support." It followed that since Unity was engaged in the same ministry as the churches, Unity should use the same methods to obtain financial support.[19]

While the Fillmores did not charge for the services of members of the Silent Unity Healing Department, they believed that these healers should be adequately compensated for their work. Writing in 1907, when the Unity movement was almost two decades old, they explained, "We are not giving out drugs, or anything that can be measured or seen, yet there is a constant outpouring of Spiritual Life Energy from this center, and all who put themselves *en rapport* with us get its effect. It has taken taken twenty years of constant work to get this current established, and we know that it is the greatest healing agent in the universe."[20]

The Fillmores believed that there should be a fair exchange between the client and healer. "Spiritual reciprocity" was the name they gave this relationship, and they defined it as "the spontaneous reciprocal exchange of values between healer

56

and patient." It was a concept that often referred to and written about. They commented:

> The healer gives his time and the word of the spirit just as fully as he knows how; this is his value. The patient is expected to give in return that which he counts valuable, be it money, jewels, books, goods or whatever.[21]

In determining how much money to give, the Fillmores asked recipients to be fair. If they were truly seeking justice they would compensate Unity healers adequately for their services. On several occasions in *Unity* magazine, the Fillmores appealed to the recipient's sense of equity:

> We appeal to your sense of justice—be fair with us. Remember that we have through years of mental experience developed the power of handling Universal Life Substance, and we pour it into your consciousness, and through it you are healed. And we have by years of study come into understanding of Divine Wisdom, which we impart to you freely. If you have made sacrifices to pay doctors, should you do anything less to pay those who place you in touch with the very elixir of life?[22]

Myrtle Fillmore felt that those engaged in healing work at Unity headquarters should have their own lives in order. Silent Unity was not a place for the psychologically needy. It was necessary, she said, that "all who engage in the work be healthy and poised, and with a faith developed to the point of handling their own personal problems, before taking up the ministry of others."[23] People who wanted to work for Unity, Myrtle insisted, must have demonstrated a capacity to give. When people apply for work with us we ask them immediately, what have you accomplished; what have you proved yourself capable of doing, what can you give?" She elaborated:

> Consecration of mind and heart, and real fitness of body, and special training are all required of those who are to taken part in the Unity work, and really do what is demanding to be done. Folks don't come here, as employees, to get something, but to give something—something fine and powerful and far-reaching. Those who come do get something, but it is after they have given, with mind and heart and physical expression.[24]

One of the more detailed accounts of the Silent Unity Healing Department—which was now beginning to be called simply Silent Unity—was written in October 1911 by Edna L. Carter, who had worked at Unity headquarters for almost a decade. In an article entitled, "Points from Silent Unity" Carter reported that the workday began early and was punctuated by periods in which all the workers gathered for silent meditation. Carter wrote:

> Every morning at ten o'clock the sixteen local workers of the Society of Silent Unity drop the letter-writing, gather in the Silence room, and join in this word: "Christ is the head of the Movement." In the afternoon at three o'clock they again have a Silence, and then spend a half hour in discussing various points that come up in the letter-writing… At five o'clock in the afternoon the regular healing silence is held.[25]

Maintaining the inner peace established during periods of silent meditation was essential in establishing proper context for the work in Silent Unity. "Everything possible is done to establish and maintain a strong healing power and atmosphere of Truth," Carter reported, "and outside thoughts were excluded as much as possible."[26] Carter then discussed the manner in which letter requests for healing were handled:

> In studying a letter preparatory to answering it, we find that we can often get the keynote to the writer's mind, that is, the letter the patient has written reveals the cause of his inharmony. When the keynote is found it is easy to give help… As a part of our study of the art of writing healing letters, some of the letters containing special problems are brought up in this three-o-clock meeting, and a general expression as to the needs of the writers comes from the workers. In this way, we get broader views and find that we help one another as well as the patients.[27]

Carter also revealed that letter-writers had been instructed not to go too deeply into the factors that my have produced ill health in the patient. She indicated: "In answering letters we often find it necessary to explain that we do not think it wise to search too much for causes of ailments. All real healing follows overcoming errors, but the error should not be emphasized in any way. Instead, it should be allowed to pass out of consciousness.[28]

Between 1910 and 1915 the Silent Unity healing work grew rapidly. Several hundred letters were now being received daily and the staff grew from twelve to thirty-five. Larger quarters were required, and space was designed specifically to meet Silent Unity's needs in a new building at Unity headquarters near downtown Kansas City. Healing was now available on a twenty-four-hour basis, including weekends, with someone available throughout the night to respond to telegrams. Details of the work were reported in the March 1915 issue of *Unity*.

The work-day began at 8:00 A.M. with a silent prayer that lasted fifteen minutes. "During the silence," it was reported, "workers sit at their desks ready to begin on their letters as soon as they have prayed for Divine Guidance and help.[29] A piece in *Weekly Unity* entitled "Facts About Silent Unity" published in March 1927 described the procedures used in handling letters:

> Each letter that is received by Silent Unity is opened and blessed. The letter is then taken to the file room where a worker looks over the records to see whether the writer has had previous correspondence with Silent Unity... When a record of the letter has been made in the file room, the letter is then prayerfully considered and answered by a Silent Unity worker who gives special attention to the case. Prayers are later offered for the writer in the Silent Unity healing meeting. Unless otherwise instructed, Silent Unity prays for its correspondents every day for thirty days.[30]

Silent Unity continued the rapid growth that began in 1910. By 1920 a total of 186,000 letters were sent out, requiring a staff of forty to process them. By 1925 the number of outgoing letters had risen to 500,000, and the staff totaled approximately sixty workers. By 1930, shortly before Myrtle's death, the workload in healing letters mailed was over 600,000, and a total of ninety healers were employed.

The increase in letters written to Silent Unity, and the staff required to answer them, was due in large part to the rapid growth of Unity's magazine publishing program. By 1928 six magazines were being published with combined circulation of 589,277 subscribers.[31] Included were: *Unity*, *Wee Wisdom*, *Weekly Unity*, *Daily Word*, *Christian Business Man* and *Youth*. Subscribers learned about Silent Unity in these publications and were moved to write for prayer and healing.

Myrtle Fillmore was close to the work of Silent Unity for four decades until her death at age eight-six in 1931. Even in her eighties, Myrtle participated in the daily healing meetings, and answered letters of those who wrote for prayer and spiritual guidance. She nurtured Silent Unity's growth from the time it was a small group of letter writers and prayer workers in the 1890s until it was a healing group ninety strong, responding to the needs of thousands of people around the world. In 1930 she described Silent Unity as "a radiant, dynamic center of spiritual life, joy, health and power."[32] Myrtle often described to her correspondents the advantages of regular contact with Silent Unity and urged them to write whenever they were in need of help. She told an acquaintance: "As you 'tune in' with Silent Unity spiritually, you are bound to be quickened, illumined, and blessed according to the needs. This mighty power station of Spirit is always in operation, and when you become receptive spiritually, you are in all ways blessed."[33]

The work of Silent Unity continued to expand after Myrtle's death. In the eighty years since her passing in 1931, millions of people from around the globe have contacted Silent Unity for prayer support, primarily by telephone. Feedback from callers indicates that their health has been renewed, their relationships have been restored and their prosperity has been increased.

## 🎕 5 🎕
# Teacher of Truth Principles

### Classroom teacher

**M**yrtle was a teacher at heart and had a burning desire to provide others with the knowledge that she herself possessed. It is not surprising that within a few years after she began working as a practitioner of spiritual healing she sought to teach others how to do the work. Both Myrtle and Charles Fillmore believed that the roles of spiritual healer and teacher were interrelated. Their ideas on the subject were expressed in the December 1, 1897 issue of Unity magazine:

Our position is that there is no permanent healing without instruction; hence we are engaged in a ministry instead of a business. If it is a ministry, then, those who invoke the healing power recognize God as its source, and upon Him they call for wisdom in their work, and unto Him they look for guidance.[1]

By 1897 they were ready to present their teaching to public audiences, and in December began teaching a two-week course (every evening Monday through Saturday at 8:00 PM) entitled "Practical Christianity and Christian Healing." The class, which had been announced in the pages of Unity magazine, drew twenty-seven students, several of whom were from outside Kansas City. Representatives from Nebraska, South Dakota, New Mexico and Indiana were in attendance. The Fillmores repeated the class several times in 1898, and for the next twelve years presented it three or four times each year at the Kansas City headquarters. While the Fillmores taught primarily in Kansas City, they traveled to Colorado to teach each August for three years (1900–1902).[2] A letter, sent from Pueblo, Colorado by Charles Fillmore to the Unity magazine staff, reported that classes were well received. He wrote:

> There are several excellent workers here, and they have all demonstrated in such a way that the doctrine has a standing among all classes. We have so far been teaching two days. Mrs. Fillmore has a morning class attended by ladies exclusively. There are about sixty in this class. She also gave a lesson at a private house in another part of the city this afternoon (August 8th) to thirty five people. I have given two evening lessons, and the church, which holds about one hundred and sixty, was comfortably full each time.[3]

In September, 1904, they were in Chicago to teach. A note from the Unity center in Chicago, printed in the October, 1904 issue of *Unity*, stated:

> Great interest is aroused in Chicago in the work being done at the Unity headquarters there. Mr. and Mrs. Fillmore are teaching a basic course, and the hall is crowded to its utmost capacity every night. It is a most appreciative and enthusiastic class, and among them are a number of prominent physicians, lawyers, ministers and businessmen. Good healing is being done and the people are thoroughly awake to the good there is for them in the Truth.[4]

A piece printed in *Unity* magazine in January, 1899, probably written by Charles, responded to questions from potential students who wanted to know more about the contents of the course and what might be gained from taking it. The article emphasized the importance of spiritual healing:

> It covers all the ground of the higher courses in practical metaphysics. We find that it is through unfoldment of degrees of the student's mind, and not from outward instruction, that understanding is attained, hence the whole aim of our method is to quicken the Spirit until it grasps for itself the Truth in all its phases. Healing is done also in connection with the instruction, and excellent results nearly always follow… It is safe to say that everyone who attends is helped in both mind and body.[5]

The January 1899 class was a particularly fruitful one. The results were reported in *Unity* magazine:

> The prime object of these lessons is to instruct students how to overcome themselves, defects of mind, body and affairs, and we have no hesitancy in saying that they are usually successful . . . It is customary on the last night to call on members of the class for testimonials and they are always interesting.[6]

Two specific examples were reported. One was of a woman who was healed of a rupture. *Unity* stated in February, 1899, that "a lady who had worn a bandage for a rupture for years, and could only go up and down stairs sideways, had found herself running up and down, and had put away her bandage."[7] Another was of a man who was apparently cured of diabetes:

> A gentleman said that this was his second class. That he joined the last April class condemned to the grave by physicians. His trouble was dia-

betes and he had tried nearly all remedies without help. He was healed
of the diabetes, but more marvelous still, one of his arms which had
been practically useless for eighteen years and was one and a half
inches shorter than the other had regained its strength, size and length.
Besides all this a defect in one eye had disappeared. The changes that
had come into his life in the short time were almost beyond his comprehension and he was not yet fully conscious of how greatly he had
been blessed.[8]

A review of the syllabus of the course indicates that the ideas Myrtle presented in her letters to correspondents and Charles covered in his lectures and
books were taught in these courses. The subjects which comprised the twelve
lessons in the course included: God, Christ, Man, Thinking, Denials and Affirmations, The Power of the Word, Spirituality, Faith and Power, Imagination,
Will and Understanding, Judgment, and Jesus and Love.[9]

## Editor "Wee Wisdom" magazine

Myrtle maintained a strong interest in the education of children, from the
time she was a school teacher in Clinton, Missouri, through her years as a
mother of three sons, and through her editorship of *Wee Wisdom* magazine.
Her decision to found Wee Wisdom as a spiritual magazine for children in 1893
was based on an inner conviction that she had an important role to play in the
spiritual education of young people. Dream images pointed the way. Children
and their needs were on her mind as she slept one evening and dreamed the
following:

> I saw many children about, with no one to get them together. I found
> myself wishing that someone would come to bring them together, and
> then someone said to me: "You made the discovery of their needs now
> you give these children what they require."[10]

Myrtle concluded that the dream had special meaning, and that Unity was
being directed to publish a magazine to fill a void in children's literature. She
recalled, "So *Wee Wisdom* came into expression to fill that place. It was a babe
born in a manger. It was wrapped in swaddling clothes." The magazine, which
appeared for the first time in August 1893, was soon to draw the help, according
to Myrtle, of "many loving friends.[11] It was Myrtle's hope that the teachings
contained in *Wee Wisdom* "would bring out the best there is in every boy and
girl." The magazine, she commented, would be addressed to children, "who

will be ready to hear and profit by the teachings of Truth in simple story and lesson form that will bring health, happiness and prosperity into [their lives]."[12] The capacity to love was one of the spiritual qualities she wanted to help; develop in her readers. She wrote, "We want to be inspired with the loving to do something for somebody, and to do this we first must find the love that is always there, and doesn't have to come and go—that love is always ready and willing."[13]

While writing and editing for the *Wee Wisdom*, Myrtle consulted her three sons who, when the magazine was first published in 1893, were eleven, nine and four. Myrtle wanted the magazine to be a participatory publication in which young readers, their parents, relatives and friends would contribute stories, poems, songs and photos. "If any little boy or girl," she asked, "has helped or healed anyone or spoken a word of Truth in a very successful way, we want them to write to us about it." She made the same request of parents. "If papa or mama who read this remember a story, song or incident that will be instructive to our little ones we should be pleased to have them send it to us. We want this paper to be cooperative."[14] Myrtle loved to get letters from her readers. "If there is anything that really does Ye Editor's heart good," she wrote, "it is these dear little letters—they bring us so close together. "Why? I can almost see and hear you when I take up your letter."[15]

The August, 1898 issue of *Wee Wisdom* contained a contribution destined to become one of Unity's most popular and well-used prayers. It was contained in a simple set of verses by Hannah More Kohaus, and it appeared in the title of "The Truth Child's Rosary." Myrtle was quick to recognize their value and told her young readers. "The six littler verses given above are for you to put on your memory string, like beads that some little children are given to count so as to help them remember things. Everyone of these six rhymes is a little prayer that will help you to remember how to be wise and brave and true and well."[16]

*God is my help in every need.*
*God does my every hunger feed.*
*God walks beside me, guides my way*
*Through every moment of the day*
*I now am wise, I now am true,*
*Patient, kind and loving too.*
*All things I am, can do, and be.*
*Through Christ, the Truth that is me.*

*God is my health, I can't be sick.*
*God is my strength, unfailing, quick.*
*God is my all; I know no fear.*
*Since God and love and Truth are here.*

While the prayer was first used to inspire children, adults found it equally appealing. Now known as "The Prayer of Faith," many use it who have no connection with Unity work.[17]

With the turn of the century her boys were no longer children. Lowell and Rickert were teenagers and Royal was soon to become one. Myrtle enjoyed involving them in the editing of *Wee Wisdom* and as they grew older she gave them full editorial responsibility for producing anniversary issues. In June 1902, in preparation for the anniversary issue which came out in August, she wrote, in her engaging style:

> We have come to the end of our sixth year together. Next month will be *Wee Wisdom*'s seventh birthday. You are all coming to celebrate it, and make it a grand success. The "Three Boys" will have charge of Ye Editor's Sanctum and will make you welcome. Be sure to come early with your letters, stories, songs and photos. The young editors have not unfolded their plans for August to me, but Wisdom will guide them, and we will have the best and brightest birthday yet."[18]

Myrtle received assistance in editing the magazine in 1907 when Blanche Sage Haseltine was brought in as an associate editor. She got further help in 1912 when Royal returned to Kansas City after graduating from the University of Missouri, and becoming managing editor. In 1913 she decided to expand the scope of the magazine to includes youths and teenagers, change the name to *Wisdom*, and give Royal expanded editorial responsibilities. She announced the change in May 1913:

> *Wee Wisdom* has for many years been going out from Unity Center each month to visit little children. But little children grow up so quickly now-a-days that *Wee Wisdom* is often left behind. Therefore *Wee Wisdom* has decided to grow up a little bit herself, so that she can help the larger children as well as do general good about the house by aiding mamma and papa in solving the little problems that come in home life.[19]

In August 1913, Myrtle gave a fuller explanation of her decision:

> Since *Wee Wisdom* made her first bow to her Wee readers, and gave them her first Truth Pillows to rest their little heads upon, the three boys who kept "Ye-editor" in sympathy with all wee folk, have grown to manhood. Even Royal, the youngest, has been home from college for two years. This fact goes to prove that generations of Wee's have risen up and passed beyond the range of *Wee Wisdom*'s ministry. So upon this, her nineteenth birthday, Royal and I have decided to celebrate through dropping the "Wee" from her name and broadening the scope of her ministry of Truth that it may include the Home and Youth as well as the Wee, and group all under the name *Wisdom*.[20]

The attempt to reach an audience of teenagers, while still addressing the needs of children, didn't work. In July, 1915, it was decided to return to the former publishing format, and revive the magazine's former name, *Wee Wisdom*. In a candid editorial note Myrtle explained why the experiment failed:

> There came a time when *Wee Wisdom* herself felt grown up and wanted a larger house in which to entertain big folks, as well as little. So she put on long dresses and grown-up ways that didn't suit her one bit. But now she has learned that the years have no power to make her older, so she has decided never to grow up, but always to be *Wee Wisdom*.[21]

Myrtle assured readers that the magazine would have a "joyful return." She told them:

> Next month we find *Wee Wisdom* with us again. She tells us that she wants to visit you just as she did before she ventured into her present work. Ye Editor, Royal, Blanche and many of her dear friends are building a new home and making beautiful dresses for her, after her original patterns.[22]

Myrtle continued as editor of the magazine until 1922 when, at age 77, she turned the editorship over to Imelda Octavia Shanklin, a long-time Unity editor and writer. The magazine grew dramatically during Myrtle's final seven years at the editorial helm. In 1916 the magazine served 4,800 subscribers. By 1922 that number has risen to 35,500.

# ❧ 6 ❧
## Charles

### Growing up in rural Minnesota

Charles was born in 1854 on an Indian reservation near St. Cloud, Minnesota, to parents who came to the state as pioneers. During his youth, his father, Henry G. Fillmore, worked as a trader with the Chippewa Indians and as a farmer. His mother, Mary Georgiana Stone Fillmore, worked as a dressmaker.[1] His parents separated when he was seven. The family was small by pioneer standards; his only sibling was a younger brother, Norton, who at age ten ran away from home.[2]

Charles grew up in a society in which educational institutions were in their infancy. The little schooling available to him as a boy was interrupted by a physically disabling accident that had life-threatening consequences. A broken hip from an ice-skating accident and improper medical treatment left him disabled physically. He reported: "When I was ten my life was crossed by what the doctors pronounced a fatal illness. It began with what was at first diagnosed as rheumatism in the right leg, which gradually developed into tuberculosis of the hip."[3] His problem was made worse by improper medical treatment from incompetent medical practitioners in a frontier community.[4]

> I was bled, leeched, cupped, lanced, seatoned, blistered and roweled. Six running sores were artificially produced on my leg to draw out the diseased condition which was presumed to be within. Physicians of different schools were employed and the last one always wondered how I ever pulled through alive under the treatment of the "quack" that preceded him; and as I look back at it now it's a miracle to me how I ever got away from them all the little bundle of bones and sinews which I found in my possession after they finished their experiments.[4]

The doctors told Charles that by the time he was forty he would be a helpless cripple in a wheelchair.[5] For several years Charles was so incapacitated that he could not lead a normal life. He explained:

> I managed after years to get on my feet, although my right leg was several inches shorter than the left, and I was to all appearances destined to chronic invalidism. I managed to get about on crutches and cane and attend school in a desultory way until I was eighteen.[6]

By the time Charles reached maturity, one leg was four inches shorter than the other and a leg brace to walk was required.[7] Religion or spirituality played practically no part in his upbringing or in his early adulthood. Though a relative on his father's side, the Reverend Glezen Fillmore, was one of the early Methodist bishops in upstate New York, his parents apparently took little or no interest in religion. Nothing in Fillmore's description of his early life indicates that he attended religious services. Indeed, he said, "I wasn't at all religious."[8]

## Business Interests in Texas and Colorado

As years passed his health improved, and when he was twenty, he decided to leave Minnesota for Texas. Evidently, the move was in part because his parents no longer lived together. "As my mother and father were separated and without a permanent home, I became restless and wanted other surroundings."[9] In 1874 he went to Paris, Texas (then Caddo in Indian territory and now in Oklahoma), where he had a cousin. Shortly thereafter, he moved to Denison, Texas, where he lived for five years, working as a clerk in the freight office of the Missouri, Kansas and Texas Railway. In 1879, Charles moved from Denison to Leadville, Colorado, where he took a course in metallurgy, became a mining assayer, and settled in Gunnison City. Evidently, things did not work out in Colorado, as a letter written in 1880 to K. Murphy, a Denison friend, indicated that life was better in Texas:

> I have not struck anything yet, and the prospects are not good for doing so either. These gold mining camps are mighty uncertain, and this one especially so. With the exception of Leadville, I have not seen a place since leaving Texas where as much business was done as in Denison. This is the most desolate, barren region. Nothing grows but sage brush and cactus. Advise your friends to stay home if they wish to be appy.[10]

In 1879, before leaving Texas for Colorado, Charles met Myrtle Page. Myrtle came to Denison, Texas in 1876 from Clinton, Missouri, where she had been teaching in the local schools. She chose Texas for reasons of health, hoping to find relief from recurring bouts of tuberculosis. She and Charles were acquainted for only a brief time before Charles left for Colorado.

Little information is available about his contact with Myrtle from mid-1879, when he moved to Colorado, and his returning to marry her in Clinton, Missouri, in the early spring of 1881. Without a doubt, they corresponded, though no copies remain of their letters. The couple left for Colorado after their marriage and settled in Gunnison. When the mining boom broke later in the year, they moved to Pueblo, where Charles engaged in real estate. It was there that Lowell and Rickert, their first two sons, were born.

## Settling in Kansas City

Charles was not ready to settle permanently in Pueblo and, in 1884, moved the family to Omaha, Nebraska. They stayed there for one year before moving on in 1885 to Kansas City. Charles attributed the constant moving to his search for his true calling:

> I never seemed satisfied with my surroundings and was not at peace with my work, and the urge to go elsewhere was always with me. So I began looking for a location, without knowing exactly where to look. We broke our home in Pueblo in 1884, and we spent one winter in Omaha, Nebraska. However, there was a constant urge to go to Kansas City, and in the spring of that year we moved.[11]

After settling in Kansas City, Charles engaged in what he called "real estate plunging," acknowledging that he was "quite successful."[12] Though living in Kansas City, he continued to maintain a financial interest in the Zuni Mining Company, which operated silver mines in western Colorado, outside the town of Silverton. Charles traveled occasionally to Silverton to involve himself in the work. The investment was a valuable one, as in 1887 he was offered $75,000 for his share.

During the mid-1880s, Charles occupied himself with business affairs, having yet to develop an interest in religion. He indicated that his early religious education was "quite limited."[13] He also said that he was "not biased on the God question by an orthodox education," and that until his mid-thirties "God was an unknown factor in my conscious mind."[14] Nothing in Charles' background prior to 1886 indicated that he would give up his business career and devote his life to spiritual teaching and healing.

It was in 1886 that he joined Myrtle in attending a series of lectures in Kansas City on spiritual healing given by E. B. Weeks, a representative of the Illinois Metaphysical College founded by Emma Curtis Hopkins. While these lectures proved to be a turning point for Myrtle, who had suffered from tuberculosis since childhood. Charles reacted to the Weeks lectures in the way a busy Kansas

City businessman might have been expected to react. "The doctrine," he said, "did not at first appeal to me."[15] However, upon seeing the physical results that Myrtle obtained in healing herself feom tuberculosis, as well as the healing work she did with Kansas City friends who became her clients, he dropped his real estate business, sometime in the late 1880s, and joined her in the work.

Growing up in Minnesota, Charles received no formal education. He never completed grade school or high school. As an adult, he supported himself and his family as a businessman, not as an editor, writer or publisher. He had no apparent experience in the work he was to pursue. It seemed apparent that the contents of Modern Thought magazine, published monthly beginning in April 1889, would reflect the qualities of an untrained, uninformed, superficial mind, considering Charles' limited educational and professional background.

Charles might be credited with being audacious but also faulted for being in over his head. Yet the range and depth of Charles Fillmore's knowledge is surprising, as revealed in the first issues of *Modern Thought* and then in the magazines that succeeded it—*Christian Science Thought, Thought, and Unity.*

He demonstrated an amazing command of the literature, from the classics of Plato, Aristotle, and Socrates to the works of William Shakespeare, William Ellery Channing, Leo Tolstoy, and Mark Twain. He had read widely in the works of the major spiritual writers of the eighteenth and nineteenth centuries, including Emanuel Swedenborg, Franz Anton Mesmer, Ralph Waldo Emerson, James Russell Lowell, Mary Baker Eddy, Warren Felt Evans, Emma Curtis Hopkins, and Ursula Gestefeld.

Charles had also delved into the literature of the occult, including hermetic philosophy, theosophy, Rosicrucianism, and spiritualism. He was well versed in the Bible as well as in the works of John Wesley and John Calvin, and he was very familiar with traditional Christian teachings. In addition, he had read the Bhagavad Gita as well as writings on Buddhism.

How did Charles amass this knowledge? We can only surmise how he acquired it. During his boyhood, after being injured in a skating accident, he was housebound and unable to attend school. However, he was able to work with a tutor who lived in St. Cloud, Minnesota, a woman by the name of Caroline (Mrs. Edgar) Taylor. She was college-educated, which was unusual for that time, and noted for her interest in classical literature. Mrs. Taylor introduced him to classics, sparked his interest in reading, taught him the rules of grammar, and gave him writing exercises.[16] Charles' phenomenal ability to synthesize, integrate, and retain the material he read can attributed to only one thing—a brilliant mind.

Charles indicated in a biographical sketch later in life that he was "self-taught."[17] He must have been a voracious reader throughout his adult years to have amassed the information that was at his fingertips when he began publishing *Modern Thought.*

Charles believed he had a mission to present a new spiritual doctrine to humankind. He stated in the inaugural issue of *Modern Thought* that the magazine would be devoted "to the development of man's devotional nature."[18] "Our aim," he said, "is to spread all over this Great West, the good which we know lies in wait for those willing to receive it."[19] Men and women needed to have a better understanding of spiritual truth: "The world must be reformed; the work is ours and we must not shrink from it."[20]

Charles told readers that the magazine would not be "an organ of any school of thought" or committed to any one doctrine, spiritual point of view, or religion. Rather, it would be of interest to "all honest souls earnestly seeking spiritual light." He believed the magazine would be of particular interest to "the independent Christian or any independent thinker on any line of spiritual philosophy or science."[21]

Charles was convinced that the religious beliefs held by traditional Christians, both Catholic and Protestant, were in large measure erroneous and were in part responsible for humankind's lack of spiritual development. Fundamentalist ministers who preach "hell-fire" and "wail over the sins of the world" had done much to poison the minds of their listeners.[22] Belief in Jesus as the Savior had caused many Christians to focus on the afterlife rather than living in the here and now. He wrote, "Thousands of so-called Christians are looking forward to death, when God is to save them into life everlasting."[23] Christians lacked self-responsibility and often saw themselves as victims. Charles observed that "Christians have leaned on others and are consequently like children in real spiritual power."[24]

Charles saw an even bigger problem with people with no religion at all, people who had succumbed to the materialism that existed in nineteenth century American society. He observed that, when people accumulated wealth, they tended to forget the needs of other less well-off members of society. "The moment man comes into earthly possessions his tendency is to selfishness, and that is the one great evil to be done away with."[25] Materialists were not aware that manifesting the divine inner presence was a life-changing possibility. In their ignorance, they worshipped a false god. As he noted in Christian Science Thought, "The most devoted worshipers at the shrine of Materialism admit that their goddess is a melancholy, dark visaged dame, continually threatening them with her cruel and vindictive temper."[26]

Charles recognized that the task he set before himself was large. "The question is," he indicated, "how can we best help humanity out of the darkness of mistaken concepts?"[27] Rather than focus on human weakness, he wanted to address human strengths, particularly the divinity he saw in all of humanity. His task was "to save men from themselves by uncovering the possibilities for good latent in every human soul—possibilities grand beyond comprehension."[28] His most bold statement regarding his mission was made in September 1893 in *Thought* magazine, where he wrote, "Our aim is to convert the world."[29]

## Organizer of Spiritual Ministries

Many spiritual leaders who excel at teaching and writing are unable to organize around their work. As a result, their teaching lasts only as long as their books are read. Charles Fillmore's work has survived him because he was a gifted organizer. He thought in terms of organization, applied business principles to spiritual practice, and brought people together in organizations for carrying on spiritual work. As a result, spiritual ministries developed around the Unity spiritual teaching.

## Metaphysical Healing

Healing others through prayer—physically, psychologically, and spiritually—has been central to Unity work from its earliest beginnings. In the spring of 1889, Charles and Myrtle Fillmore began praying with people, both individually and at distance, as practitioners of what they ultimately called metaphysical healing. At the outset of their work in the 1890s Charles organized two groups for the purpose of absent healing, The Society of Silent Unity and the Silent Unity Healing Department.

The work of the Society of Silent Unity was begun in April 1890. Initially called the Society of Silent Help, the organization's name was changed in June 1891 to the Society of Silent Unity with the founding of *Unity* magazine. The Society's purpose was to foster the expansion of Charles and Myrtle's teaching and healing work beyond Kansas City.[30]

Growing up alongside the Society of Silent Unity in their Kansas City headquarters was the Silent Unity Healing Department. This group's name was ultimately changed to "Silent Unity." Information on the growth and development of Silent Unity and absent healing is contained in Chapter Three, "Silent Unity."

## Publishing

The formation of the Society of Silent Unity and the Silent Unity Healing department were the result of Charles' ability as an organizer. The same could be said for the publishing program that began in 1889 with *Modern Thought* magazine, and was followed in 1890 by Thought magazine, and then in 1891 with *Unity* magazine which continues to be published to this day. In 1893 Wee Wisdom magazine was introduced, and edited by Myrtle. The production and promotion of *Wee Wisdom* would not have been possible without the business management skills of Charles.

The Unity Tracy Society which Charles established in 1897 published a sizeable number of books and pamphlets, primarily by well-known metaphysical authors or by members of the Kansas City Unity staff or by Unity center leaders around the country. In July 1915 *Unity* magazine listed a total of 125 tracts in print and in September 1917 reported that the number of copies printed between 1915 and 1917 was 1,478,150. In April 1923, Unity reported that three million copies of tracts were published that year.[31]

The most successful book published by the Unity Tracy Society was Lessons in Truth by Emilie Cady, a New York City homeopathic physician. It was a popular favorite within the Unity Movement throughout the twentieth century and into the twenty first. By the year 2010 it had been translated into several languages and sales totaled over 1.6 million copies.

During the first three decades of the twentieth century, several new magazines were introduced under Charles' leadership. *Weekly Unity*, begun in 1909 and edited by Charles and Myrtle's eldest son, Lowell, became a highly successful publication, ultimately outdistancing Unity magazine in circulation. In the 1920s Weekly Unity serviced over 100,000 subscribers. Daily Word was begun in 1925. Edited by Frank B. Whitney, a talented young Silent Unity worker, it was to surpass in readership all magazines published by Unity. The Christian Business Man was introduced in 1922 and presented short articles that taught the practice of Christian psychology in business. Youth magazine was founded in 1926, and was aimed at an audience of young readers who had outgrown *Wee Wisdom*.

Charles Fillmore's first book, and one of his most important, was *Christian Healing*, published in 1909. This and the other books he wrote, and ultimately published through the Unity School of Christianity, most likely would have never seen the light of day had he not created in 1897 a book publishing organization, the Unity Tract Society. It is highly unlikely that a commercial publisher would have been interested in any of his works.

In addition to *Christian Healing*, he is the author of *Talks on Truth*, *The Twelve Powers of Man*, *Metaphysical Bible Dictionary*, *Prosperity*, *Mysteries of Genesis*, *Jesus Christ Heals*, *Teach us to Pray* (co-authored with Cora Dedrick Fillmore) and *Mysteries of John*. Three books were published posthumously, *Atom Smashing Power of Mind* and *Keep as True Lent* again through the help of Cora.

## Spiritual Education

During the 1890s, classes and workshops in "Practical Christianity" were taught by Charles and Myrtle in Kansas City, and were the primary means for educating Unity students. These classes they said, "covered all the ground of the higher courses in Metaphysics."[32] In 1901 they began a course which they called ''Advanced Course in Concentration." In addition they offered a course in "Christian Living and Healing."

They continued this work until 1909 when, in an effort to reach students outside Kansas city, they created a course in Unity teaching that could be taken by correspondence.[33] This led to the establishment of the Unity Correspondence School, another of the organization innovations of Charles Fillmore. The correspondence course was immediately popular with Unity students. By June 1909, 268 students were enrolled.[34] By November the total had risen to seven hundred[35]; and at the end of the first year, (March 1910) over nine hundred pupils were taking the courses.[36] Enrollment continued to grow, and in addition to students throughout the United States, there were enrollments from Cuba, Brazil, England, Scotland, France Germany, Russia, India, Japan and Australia. Within a short time the correspondence course became the basic text for the Unity teachings, and was recommended for all who wished to become teachers and healers.[37]

## Unity Centers

Unity centers for teaching, healing, and weekly religious services began germinating in the mind of Charles Fillmore in the early 1890s. After being ordained by Emma Curtis Hopkins of the Theological Seminary of Chicago,

Charles spoke periodically on Sundays in the early 1890s as a part of the "No Name Lecture Series," sponsored by the Christian Science association of Kansas City.[38] He began organizing religious services on Sundays with Myrtle for the first time in 1894. These first meetings, referred to as "Unity meetings," were devoted primarily to Bible study. All meetings were open to the public.[39]

By 1896, these Sunday meetings were held in a room adjacent to Unity headquarters in the Pythian building on Walnut street in Kansas City. The "order of exercises" contained many of the elements found in traditional Christian services of the Protestant variety—silent prayer, scripture reading, congregational singing, silent meditation, and Bible study.[40] In June 1897, the Sunday meetings were held under the auspice of the Unity Society of Practical Christianity. It was the first time the society was identified in Unity magazine as the organizing group for these meetings, called "Sunday services." Services were conducted both on Sunday and during the week in facilities that could hold about one hundred people.[41]

In 1903, the Unity Society for Practical Christianity was incorporated "for scientific and educational purposes," under the laws of Missouri. The development of the first Unity center, which functioned much like a church, would not have been accomplished without the leadership and organizational ability of Charles Fillmore.

With the success of the Unity center in Kansas City, Charles began encouraging Unity students outside the city to emulate the local work and start Unity centers in their communities. Center leaders were provided with a variety of services that included helpful literature from Unity publications, course work by correspondence from the Unity Correspondence School, and publicity in towns and cities where Unity centers were located. In addition, potential center leaders were invited to come to Kansas City and take classes in Practical Christianity.

In summary, Charles' contribution to the organization of Unity centers as spiritual ministries consisted of planning and organizing the first Unity center in Kansas City, initiating the work that established centers outside Kansas City, and setting in motion the work that was ultimately performed by the Unity Training School, the Unity Ministers Association, established in 1946, and the association of Unity Churches, founded in 1966. This organizational work that Charles fostered was outside Myrtle's interests or capabilities.

## Unity School of Christianity

During the 1890s, Unity work—the Unity ministries of publishing, prayer, religious services and spiritual education—were administered by Charles under various organizational umbrellas. Shortly after the turn of the century, in 1903, under Charles' leadership, the Kansas City Unity Society of Practical Christianity was incorporated. It managed four Unity groups: the Unity center Sunday services in Kansas City, publishing, Silent Unity Prayer work, and spiritual education. In 1909 Unity magazine began referring to the "Unity Society," as the organizational designation for these ministries.[42]

Though it had no official legal status, the "Unity Society" by 1910 had become the preferred organizational designation for the Unity movement. In a Sunday morning address on November 24, 1910 titled "What Has the Unity Society to Be Thankful For" Charles emphasized the steady growth in all aspects of the work and the impact of the teaching:

> Other societies had outstripped us from the worldly point of view, but we are satisfied to know that there has been here planted a great Truth that shall never pass away, but shall grow and be given to the whole earth. We have established here a school which is founded on Principle."[43]

In April 1913, Weekly Unity referred to the Unity Society as a "school" rather than a religious organization, indicating that a new designation for Unity work was in the offing:

> The Unity Society is not a church, but a school for the training and discipline of all who would develop spiritually. It aims especially to prepare teachers for the work of spreading the Truth. In keeping therefore, with our mission, every session should bear out the school idea and each member of the various classes should enter heartily into his privileges as a student.[44]

By 1914 Charles had concluded that the name "Unity Society" did not accurately reflect the nature of the Unity work. Since Unity had become an institution with a major interest in spiritual education in a Christian context, the name "Unity School of Christianity" seemed to be a better fit for Unity work. The September 1914 issue of *Unity* described the purposes of the new organization:

To establish and maintain a school, institute or college for the instruc-tion and promotion of mental, moral, spiritual and physical principles and qualifications deemed best for the promotion of the harmony, health, and happiness of mankind, and to apply such principles and qualifications to such purposes as healing diseases and ailments any-where.[45] The school, which was incorporated under the General and Business Corporation Act of Missouri on April 14, 1914, included within its organizational structure the Unity Tract Society, the Society of Silent Unity, the Silent Unity Healing Department, the Unity Correspondence School, the Silent-70, and the Unity Pure Food Company.[46] With incorporation in 1914 of the Unity School of Chris-tianity, all of the organizational entities Charles created—the prayer, publishing and spiritual education ministries, as well as the supporting services for Unity centers outside Kansas City—were brought together under one organizational unit.

## Marital and work relationship with Myrtle

It appears that as Charles and Myrtle began working together as practitioners of mental healing the nature of their marital relationship changed. Myrtle no longer played the subservient role of wife and mother. She was much more assertive when she and Charles became equal partners in developing and advancing the teaching, taught classes in Practical Christianity together as co-equals, and shared the same speaker's platform for Sunday services. Myrtle gave the meditation and Charles the sermon. A regular attendee at their Sunday serv-ices testified that Myrtle was never just a part of the supporting cast. He wrote:

> For many years Myrtle Fillmore took more than half the time allotted to the Sunday morning lecture. Many times I have sat in the audience and heard Mr. Fillmore remark at the close of her talk that it was time to close the service and that he would just add a few closing remarks for his sermon.[47]

She did not take a back seat when classes were being taught. This same Unity student observed:

> She taught classes and often when she attended classes of other teach-ers she would almost take over the class because she was so filled with the desire to expound the Truth as she saw it.[48]

Myrtle's secretary lent support to the view that, when it came to articulating the contents of the Unity teaching, Myrtle refused to take a back seat to Charles. The long-time Unity editor and teacher, Martha Smock, testified:

> Myrtle's secretary says that Myrtle always sat in the front row when Mr. Fillmore was teaching classes, usually with her eyes closed. But, if Charles said something with which she disagreed, she would speak out and challenge his view.[49]

Smock also reported on how Myrtle, on occasion, would keep Charles in tow at Sunday services:

> Those who used to attend their Sunday and Wednesday services recall how they sat in two high-backed chairs on the platform. Mr. Fillmore always wore a coat with rather long tails. If he talked too long Mrs. Fillmore would reach up and pull his coattails. He never seemed to mind, and enjoyed a laugh with the congregation.[50]

Charles recognized that Myrtle's participation was essential in their 1890s bootstrap operation and, in an interview conducted by Charles Brodie Patterson for *Mind* magazine in 1902, gave full credit to Myrtle for her contribution in getting the thirteen-year-old Unity movement off the ground. Charles remarked:

> Encouraged by my wife, I persevered when almost at the point of failure; and if there comes any universal success out of this continuous effort she should have the greater share of the credit. Had I been alone I would more than once have thrown the whole thing over and gone back to my real estate business.[51]

One might expect to find examples of discord in the relationship of two strong-minded people who lived and worked together for over fifty years. Myrtle's vast correspondence indicates that they saw eye-to-eye on spiritual matters, worked well together, respected each other, and enjoyed each other's company. If there was discord or disagreement, or if they fought with each other, they made no public demonstration of it. Since the two were seldom apart from the time they began Unity work in 1889 until Myrtle died in 1931, there was little written correspondence between them which might shed more light on how they related to each other.

The one exchange of letters that does exist dates to August, 1909, when Myrtle had traveled alone to Manitou, Colorado, probably to teach, visit friends and get away from the hot Kansas City summer. Charles, as was his habit, remained in Kansas City. The letters demonstrate the warmth of affection that existed between the two. In a letter written August 18th she tells him how she wished he was there. "I think of you at home… I'd love you all to be here. I thought how much the boys would have enjoyed the trip (into the mountains) yesterday." She then told him how a woman psychic sensed him in the room. "It was just as if you came in and wanted to see how we were getting along. She says it was as clear to her as if you'd really come in person." Myrtle noted that she felt they were continually together in spirit, despite the miles between them. "Of course, I know you are with us in thought very often. And we are always together in soul." She closed the letter "with love and blessings."[52]

Four days later on August 22nd, Charles' 55th birthday, she wrote to tell him how important he was to her:

> I wrote you this morning and wanted so much to have something to send you that would express my appreciation of this date. And lo tonight it came about that I could do so. The little package I am sending you, is a demonstration—and though you don't generally care for jewels you will always love to wear this, for it is a genuine rub and is your birth stone, and glows with the warmth and love of August—as well as symbolizes a love that never grows cold or faileth.[53]
>
> From your old pard and lover,

Two letters from Charles to Myrtle while she was in Colorado, are still in existence, and both explain that he was too tied down with work at Unity headquarters to make the trip to Colorado. On August 20th he reported: "Your first letter came this A.M. Royal read me the letter while I was in bed. It was almost as good as being there myself." He then told her that getting away from Kansas City would be difficult because of work he had to do—letters to answer, a sermon to write, and a magazine to get out. He signed the letter, "With oceans of love, Your Charles"[54] He wrote again two days later, saying that Lowell believed he could get away for a few days, but he thought it hardly worth while. He signed this letter "With a whole lot of love, Charles."[55]

As years passed Myrtle took occasional trips outside Kansas City—she traveled with her youngest son Royal to New York in 1915 and to Canada in

1923—but seldom with Charles. In 1928 she was invited to come to California by a friend. She really wanted to go, but as had been the case in the past, could not convince Charles to travel. Her response indicated that Charles was reluctant to leave Kansas City because he hadn't finished the healing work on his leg and hip. She wrote:

> I must confess your letter has given me quite a thrill! And, like a little girl, I hurried to show it to Mr. Fillmore, to see what he thought about the idea of our flying across country! And, would you believe it—he isn't at all enthusiastic about flying! I have tried, ever so many times, to get him to join me in a lovely trip somewhere. But the dear man just doesn't like to get out among crowds; and really feels that he'd rather wait until he has completed his demonstration of healing his leg before going out, either for lecture work or pleasure.[56]

While Myrtle and Charles were fully absorbed in Unity work they occasionally found time to go to the movies, attend a play, or take in a musical event. After seeing the opera "The Ring of the Nibelungs" with Charles, Myrtle commented, "We folks of the present day have become so used to the movies and the quick action and all, that we need re-education to enjoy the long sitting of an opera, like this one." After attending "The Passion Play" with Charles she noted that while "neither one of us understand the German tongue," they still enjoyed it. "The artists acted their parts very well indeed, and the play was well worth seeing."[57]

The Unity School social functions were a continuing source of diversion and pleasure. As the staff grew in size (it was at 500 when Myrtle died in 1931) there were picnics at Unity farm, parties on special occasions, concerts by the Unity band and plays put on by Unity workers themselves. The Fillmores were often in attendance. Unity workers, who were rewarded by management for outstanding performance with theater tickets, often attended with them. Myrtle described one of these occasions to a friend:

> Mr. Fillmore and I are very busy every day; but today some of our Unity workers invited us to join with them in a well-earned good time. The team that won the perfect attendance record for the year are being treated to a good show, and they insisted that we should go with them and share the fun.[58]

Myrtle's description of a Valentine's Day party they attended is probably indicative of the pleasure they got in participating in many similar social occasions. She wrote:

> **We are going to have a little Valentine party tomorrow, and Mr. Fillmore and I have been invited to attend. We are going to be the Mamma and Pappa, you know. There will be a luncheon at Unity Inn, and we'll have a jolly good time I expect.**[59]

As the Unity movement became world-wide and the number of employees in Kansas City grew into the hundreds, Myrtle and Charles continued to behave as if they, and the workers at Unity headquarters, were a part of a community rather than a business. Eric Butterworth, a long-time Unity minister, commented on how they handled themselves at lunch-time at the Unity Inn:

> **I was always impressed to see Charles and Myrtle in line at mealtimes, like everybody else. They would take their place with their trays and proceed step by step, no matter how long the lines, and sometimes it was very long. Unless you knew who they were you would never imagine that those two people were the founders of Unity… It is such a human thing, and so natural that you had to really think about it to realize that Charles and Myrtle were not being 'democratic' as people say nowadays when executives meet with employees. These two were simply being the warm, friendly, unostentatious human beings that they were at heart. They were simply being themselves, and that was that.**[60]

The Fillmores also continued to acknowledge that their own spiritual transformation was still in process, and that more inner work needed to be done. Myrtle wrote to a friend, "Mr. Fillmore and I are seeking to sluff off every old thought habit, and every ounce of excess baggage, whether manifest or mental, so that we may run forward joyously."[61] In the evening after work Myrtle liked to share with Charles some of the more interesting letters she received during the day. Charles often had a comment, or a word of advice, which Myrtle relayed back to her correspondent.

Myrtle, who had a talent for identifying promise in spiritually inclined young men, corresponded for a time with a young poet by the name of Lawrence. She enjoyed the spiritual nature of his poetry and dubbed him "Saint Lawrence." She addressed him that way in all of her correspondence. One evening she shared some of his writing with Charles. She then responded to Saint Lawrence with these comments:

> Your message of beauty and nature and soul appreciation came a few weeks ago. I shared it with Mr. Fillmore. I think he'd never read your letters before. He's not a gusher, but I was delighted to hear his comments. He said, "Why, that man is a poet." Of course it was not news to me, for I put a laurel on you when I sainted you."[62]

She told her close friend, Laura Bolles, who was on a trip abroad, about how much Charles enjoyed her travel letters. She wrote:

> Your delightful, descriptive letters telling about all the new and wonderful things you are finding in the world beyond the ocean are being hungrily devoured by all of us. Mr. Fillmore reads every one of them eagerly and enthusiastically.[63]

Sometimes Charles had words of advice, which Myrtle passed on, as in the case of a woman who was being abused by her husband. Myrtle told her, "Mr. Fillmore has read your letter too, and his counsel is, 'get the best lawyer you can, and proceed with the divorce'."[64]

One of the fashionable things women did in the 1920s was to bob their hair. For some time Charles had wanted Myrtle to put her hair up in a bob, but she resisted. Finally, one day while at the hair dresser she got a "bob", not by choice, however. She explained to a friend how it happened, and reported Charles' reaction:

> Now that you've told of your bobbed hair, I'll have to confess that I at present have bobbed hair, too! Not by choice, however, and in fact, my vanity suffered a bit when I found out that I was bobbed. My hair had been coming out badly, and I asked my hairdresser to trim some of it off—thinking to protect and keep what I had, while the new hair was coming in. And she gave me a rather short bob! Mr. Fillmore was delighted. He had tried to have my hair bobbed a number of times.[65]

A particularly joyous occasion for them was the celebration of their golden wedding anniversary on March 29, 1931. They told a few friends about the occasion, but planned no big celebration. The 29th fell on a Sunday, and when they walked into the chapel for Sunday service at 9th and Tracy, Ernest Wilson, the Editor of Youth magazine and an ordained minister, was waiting for them at the front of the congregation. To their surprise and delight, Wilson performed the Unity marriage ceremony for them. She expressed her appreciation for the occasion in her comments to her long-time friend Kate Heffelfinger:

> We were quite satisfied with the fifty-year knot that had held out so well, but this new ceremony makes it time-proof. So much love and so many rich blessings have come to us on the occasion of our half-century anniversary, that all wealth will last until our one-hundredth celebration. When Jesus increased the loaves and the fishes to feed the multitude there were twelve baskets left over. So our running over measure will last for at least another half-century.[66]

Myrtle often drew upon her own experience as a marital partner in advising others how to succeed in relationships with significant others. Her views on the spiritual nature of relationships was made clear in the following comments to a correspondent. She wrote:

> The purpose of human relationships is the glorification of the divine. The purpose of life is to manifest God...The only true, lasting relationships are those on the spiritual plane.[67]

# ❧ 7 ❧
# *Early Years*

## *From Ohio to Missouri*

Myrtle's early years gave no indication that someday she would lead a world-wide spiritual movement that would attract thousands to its teaching. Born August 6, 1845, almost two decades before the Civil War, she was the seventh of Marcus and Lucy Page's eight children. Her father was a moderately successful Ohio farmer.

Myrtle (she was christened Mary Caroline Page) was bright, and from an early age was a curious child who loved learning:

> I remember my school days and my eagerness to read and learn what others knew. I always wanted to read the books that were supposed to be for big boys and the grown-ups, but little girls were not encouraged to such reading, so I had to take my brother's books quietly and go secretly to a little corner to enjoy them.[1]

As she grew older her reading tastes expanded. "I liked the old myths, fairy tales, histories and scientific words," she recalled. " I have found that those stories, and the visions of scientists of those days and of hundreds of years ago, all have to do with our present-day life."[2]

Her parents were devoted to Christianity, not the more liberal kind Myrtle was later to practice, but the strict Methodist variety, with its puritanical moral code and its belief in a punishing God. From an age Myrtle was repulsed by the Methodist teaching on the nature of God:

> I found my dear ones did not have an understanding of God, who ruled in their lives, which satisfied me… My mother was a very spiritual woman. She always kept the principles of right and wrong before us by her own example. But she accepted the church creed. And had such a devotional spirit that she felt that if her God saw fit to punish, or do any of the many things that were attributed to God, he must have reason for it and it was all right. I marveled that my wonderful mother, who loved so devotedly, could have a God who might punish, or take the lives of his children.[3]

Unlike most of her Christian contemporaries, she was repelled by puritanical teachings on sin and the nature of evil. "There was something in me that protested against the declaration that I was by nature evil and sinful."[4]

Disease lay like a dark cloud over much of her youth. She was afflicted at a young age by tuberculosis. Family members on her father's side had been stricken with it, and Myrtle assumed that she contracted it because TB ran in the family. She went through several bouts of illness during her childhood and youth. She reported:

> **During my childhood there was no real understanding of God as the health of his people. And so, I did not know how to disconnect myself from the hereditary thought of weakness… I may not have had what a child should have to enable it develop a sturdy body.**[5]

She was able, however, to finish high school and hold down a job as a writer for a newspaper in Columbus, Ohio. At age twenty-one she enrolled in "The Literary Course for Ladies" at Oberlin College. The program lasted for one year, as women were not eligible for the four-year degree program available for men. Upon finishing in 1867 she received a teaching license, and the following year accepted a job teaching in the public school in Clinton, Missouri, a small town about 60 miles southeast of Kansas City. Except for a year in Denison, Texas in 1877 and 1878, recovering from tuberculosis, she spent the next thirteen years teaching in the Clinton school system. She had family in Clinton, a brother David, and a sister, whose name she doesn't disclose in her letters, also lived in Clinton.

She found teaching highly rewarding, "What a joy it was to me to come in touch with those young folks, and helped them to hitch their wagons to stars, and to keep their eyes toward the heights." She delighted in "talking over their dreams and praising their efforts, and bringing to their notice the best literature and other arts."[6]

## From Clinton to Kansas City

Myrtle met Charles Fillmore in Denison, Texas, where she had gone to get relief from a bout with tuberculosis. Their correspondence does not pin down the date when they met or the circumstances. The two existing pieces of correspondence between them in 1878 indicate they were in the early stages of getting to know each other when Myrtle left Denison in the late summer of 1878 to resume teaching in Clinton, Missouri. On July 16, 1878, a few weeks before Myrtle left Denison, Charles sent her a note, friendly but business-like in tone, that acknowledged the return of a book by James Russell Lowell. He addressed her as "Miss Page" rather than "Myrtle," indicating that their relationship had not advanced to the point where he felt comfortable addressing her in a more familiar way. He also enclosed "a little light literature" which he thought she might enjoy. He remarked, "I have been quite thoughtful in my selections—including both religious and secular."[7]

On September 1, 1878, in response to a letter from Charles suggesting that they correspond, Myrtle replied from Clinton, more as an acquaintance than as a person with whom a deep bond of friendship had been established. She did not address him as "Charles," as she did in later correspondence, but as "Mr. Fillmore." Nothing in her letter indicates that an intimate relationship had developed. Myrtle replied:

> I was truly pleased to find, when I returned from my visit in the country Thursday, among my other mail, a letter from you. Such a correspondence would prove rather a treat than a burden to me. I shall ever be grateful to you for contributing so much to my literary enjoyments, and for new thoughts, suggestions—yes, and for a kind of sympathy I seldom meet.[8]

She then made a statement indicating that, before she left Denison, their acquaintance had been brief. She wrote, "How much more enjoyable my winter would have been in Texas had I known you." In his letter Charles asked her about her religious beliefs, indicating that the two had not yet spent sufficient time together to explore in depth the question of spirituality. She responded,

> You question my *orthodoxy*? Well, if I were called upon to write an outline of my creed it would be rather a strange mixture. I am decidedly *eclectic* in my theology—is it not my right to be? Over all is a grand ideal God but full of love and mercy—And dear to my heart is Christ—the perfect man who shared our earthly sorrows—yet ever lived blameless and taught such sweet lessons of patience, forgiveness, and tolerance. Outside of ourselves must we go for a strength to trust—and rely on and trusting that strength proves a help—call it what name you choose—the soul understands it.[9]

Charles evidently felt self conscious about his deformed hip and leg, and mentioned it in his letter. Myrtle made suggestions as to how he might revise his thinking on the matter. She said:

Now let me as a friend, beg of you not to let "that cloud" you speak of shut the sunshine out of your life. You are too sensitive about it. Believe me, those worthy of your friendship do not notice so small a defect. Think what is it to a moral or spiritual deformity! And how many such we meet daily. Remember this whenever you see some poor disfigured soul peer out of a sad face. And thank God, for a physical ill.[10]

Myrtle also commented on the books they had exchanged before she left Denison for Clinton:

I am glad you enjoyed "Getting on in the World." Am in no hurry for the book. If you find anyone else it may benefit, let them read it. How do you like Shelley? I am reading the second volume of "The Soul of Things" but I'll not comment now."[11]

Myrtle closed the letter as a friend might. She said: "I shall be glad to hear from you anytime. Very truly your friend, Myrtle Fillmore." When they met in 1878, Charles Fillmore was only twenty-four, considerably younger than the thirty-three year old Myrtle, and considerably less educated. She was college trained and had worked twelve years as a school teacher. His schooling had been spotty, due to illness as a teenager. He never finished high school and was working as a railway freight clerk, having come to Texas from Minnesota when he was twenty.

It would be two and a half years before they would marry. Little is known about their courtship as only one letter from the period survives, and that was written just ten days before their wedding. Myrtle was in Clinton teaching until their marriage on March 29, 1881, and Charles divided his time between Denison, Texas, and Gunnison, Colorado. In August, 1879, Charles visited Fillmore family relatives in Valparaiso, Indiana, but there is no indication he stopped in Clinton to see Myrtle.[12]

Sometime in 1879, probably late summer or fall, he went to Leadville, Colorado, where he took a course in metallurgy. He then located for a time in Gunnison. Little information is available on his activities and none regarding his connection with Myrtle until March, 1881. Charles gave only the sketchiest details of his life during this period. He wrote:

In 1879 I went to Leadville, Colorado where I took a course in metallurgy and became a mining assayer, and then located in Gunnison. In 1880 I went back to Denison, Texas. In the spring after that year I met Miss Page at her home town, Clinton, Missouri, where we were married, after which we went directly to Gunnison, Colorado, our home for a season.[13]

Ten days before their marriage, on March 19, 1881, Myrtle wrote Charles who was in Denison. This letter indicates that Myrtle was in Denison in late winter 1881, and spent time with Charles. It can be inferred from the letter they made the decision to marry during her stay there. Myrtle left Denison by train for Clinton in mid-March. On her trip north she was accompanied by a man with whom she had been previously involved romantically, and who had been trying to win her back. She told Charles:

> The offended propriety you left on the train set its blood mounted face hard to the north. Denison faded—so did the indignant color, but the crime remained on record and the criminal was brought to trial. It lasted the length of my journey and was clearly proven that the accused not only had in his possession invaluable property of mine but that he is invested with an "Open Sesame" that renders powerless the locks and keys of my treasure house. It is further shown that I have no defense against him… It seems that man I once had faith in has been visiting his old home since his widowhood—with my letters pressed to his heart—and that he has found consolation in publishing. That if Myrtle Page did not marry him she had never loved anyone else—and prided himself in that I would never marry. I tell you this for it has stirred such a feeling of pity in me—that a heart (I had thought) so noble could carry love to such a pitiful depth. (It was a tear, but only of pity.) Sister tells me he has been sending papers here to me since my stay in the south—papers filled with his literary efforts—but that brother Dave burned or gave them away so that they might not reach me.[14]

She then told Charles how glad she was to rid of her former lover, and how things would change after they were married:

> The next two weeks will put an end to his foolish egotism—he will learn that Myrtle Page *can love again* and those old letters will fall gray ashes at his feet. It is "my good angel" that has saved me. Know this. I have no regrets—there is pity, that is all.[15]

She also let Charles know how important he had become to her, although there are no details as to what transpired to make this happen:

> Who would believe it, the good friends that flock to see me do not satisfy as they did six months ago. With shame-facedness I must confess there is but *one* that sounds the measure of my happiness. Are you satisfied with your power—that brought my proud spirit to confess you are a need to it? I did not realize this fully till I found myself carried away from you. And now I am glad that the time is short before your coming.[16]

Apparently there was some urgency in their marrying and leaving quickly for Colorado. Myrtle, who was teaching in Clinton, obviously had to give up her position in the middle of the term. A summer wedding would have avoided that. Charles, who traveled to Clinton from Denison, would spend no more than 24 hours there before the marriage. In her March 19th letter Myrtle referred to the fact that Charles would be leaving Denison for Clinton on Monday, March 28th. It is probable, given the distance between Denison and Clinton, he did not arrive until late that day or possibly the morning of the 29th, the day of the wedding. Further evidence that Charles was still in Denison, just two days before they were married, is contained in a note, penned by a friend by the name of Mollie Rose, who, on Sunday, March 27th, wrote the following message in Charles' autograph book:

> As the coming years glide swiftly down the stream of time, may these be recorded as each "Page" of your life history, volumes of advancement and success, and every "Myrtle" wreath of love and happiness, daily crown your life with all that is bright and beautiful.[17]

The marriage ceremony was scheduled for the evening of Tuesday the 29th. It was to take place in the home of a friend rather than in a church; only a few people would be present; no reception was planned and the couple planned to leave that night for Colorado shortly after exchanging vows. The Clinton papers reported the brief details:

> Fillmore-Page in Clinton, Tuesday evening, March 29, 1881, at the residence of Mr. J. G. Vinson by Dr. S. Jones—Mr. Charles Fillmore of Gunnison City, Colorado, to Miss Myrtle Page of Clinton. The ceremony was witnessed only by a few friends of the contracting parties,

and the bride and groom left at 9 p.m. for Colorado, their future home.[18]

The couple lived only a few months in the frontier town of Gunnison. "The mining boom broke," recalled Charles, "and, seeking new pastures, we moved to Pueblo, Colorado, where I engaged in the real-estate business."[19] Myrtle was pregnant at the time with their first son, Lowell, who was born January 4, 1882. Two and one-half years later, on June 1, 1884, Waldo Rickert was born in Pueblo. The family left Colorado for Kansas City—with a brief stop in Omaha—shortly after Rickert was born. Charles explained the reasons for their frequent moves and their reason for finally choosing Kansas City:

> I never seemed satisfied with my surroundings nor at peace with my work, and the urge to go elsewhere was always with me. So I began looking for a location, without knowing exactly where to look. We broke up our home in Pueblo in 1884, and we spent one winter in Omaha, Nebraska. However, there was a constant inner urge to go to Kansas City.[20]

Charles evidently made a significant amount of money in Kansas City soon after arriving. He reported, "The first few years here were spent in real-estate 'plunging' in which I was quite successful.[21] A Kansas City newspaper gave an indication of the size of his holdings when it reported, "Mr. Fillmore accumulated $150,000 in real estate business here." A sum of $150,000 was a tidy amount in the 1880s. In 2010 dollars it would be well over $1,000,000.

During the first five years of their marriage (1881–1886) Myrtle was preoccupied with raising her two young sons. She had the help of her mother-in-law Mary Georgiana Fillmore, (Momsey) who had lived with Charles in Denton, Texas, and who evidently moved in with them shortly after they were married.

Letters from Myrtle to Charles, written from Clinton, where on occasion she visited family in 1885 and 1886, are full of news about the boys and show that her attention was focused on their care and well-being. Her positive attitude towards child-raising, which was so apparent after she immersed herself in Truth principles, was not in evidence in a letter written to Charles on March 1, 1885. Ricker was about nine months old at the time and Lowell had just turned three. Referring to Rickert, Myrtle complained:

> He is such a load and so restless to be on his feet, my poor back is nearly broken. Sometime I scarcely get up and down, it hurts so. If

there was only someone to relieve me an hour or two a day, or keep him till I got a little rest… He is not in the least might sick, but just restless. Too much vitality for his poor mother these days. These boys consume every bit of my time every day. I do not leave him for a moment—can't find any place that is safe to hold him, can scarcely hold him myself. I won't let him creep—tis too cold and dirty for that.[22]

Her comments, in describing her response to a visit with a sick friend, also indicates that she had yet to learn how to handle a reactive mind, and had yet to develop her ability to deal with fear and negative thought. She wrote to Charles:

I got an hour's leave of absence in the P.M. and ran down to see Fannie De la Vergue who has been sick with low fever. After my return a feeling of such terrible worry and distress of mind came over me. I was (so) distracted I could not shake it off. I could not reason myself out of it—and that night after all were in bed I walked the floor in agony and prayed. I went to bed in distress of mind which gradually gave way to sleep. When I awoke in the morning the burden seemed lifted. I have had no such terrible pressure of mind since. I have had it before and even worse.[23]

While Myrtle was in Clinton in March, 1885, her brother tried to persuade her to convince Charles to move the family to Clinton. "He has several times referred to the topic," she wrote. Myrtle considered it a poor idea. "I don't think you would like so small a place," she predicted, "and I do not want a home here for several reasons, one of which is its malarious diseases."[24]

During the early years of their marriage Myrtle suffered from recurring bouts of tuberculosis. Her son Lowell's testimony indicated the seriousness of her condition. Writing years later he reported:

I did not realize at that time that my mother's health was in a very critical condition… I have since learned that my mother in those early days was in the advanced stages of tuberculosis, and that the doctors had given her only a few months to live. She was always cheerful and never seemed to be unhappy, so I did not realize that she was ill.

Lowell attributed his mother's poor health in part to her beliefs. She had long held the conviction that she had inherited her tuberculosis from her father.

"Therefore," surmised Lowell, she "accepted her condition as hopeless."[25] Myrtle's condition was sufficiently acute to cause the Fillmores to consider leaving Kansas City. Charles remembered: "The tubercular trouble with which Mrs. Fillmore had suffered from childhood became so aggravated that nothing availed, and we were considering returning to the mountains as a last resort."[26] They stayed because of a message Charles received, contained in a dream. He recalled:

> Then I had a strange dream. An unseen voice said, "Follow me." I was led up and down the hilly streets of Kansas City and my attention was called to localities that I was familiar with. The Presence stopped and said, "You will remember having had a dream some years ago in which you were shown this city and told that you had a work to do here. Now you are being reminded of that dream and also informed that the invisible power that has located you will continue to be with you and your appointed work." When I awoke I remembered that I had had such a dream and forgot it. Then we made Kansas City our permanent home.[27]

Charles' dream coincided with a course of lectures he and Myrtle were to attend on spiritual healing which were to have a major impact on their lives. Charles explained the sequence of events: "About at this time Dr. E. B. Weeks, a representative of the Illinois Metaphysical College founded by Emma Curtis Hopkins, came here from Chicago and gave a course of lessons which Mrs. Fillmore and I attended." The impact was immediate on Myrtle. Charles continued:

> Mrs. Fillmore caught the idea that God was the source of her life and that she did not have to suffer the ills of her ancestors. Her healing began at once, and in about a year she was in good health and began healing her neighbors.[28]

Myrtle's health evidently improved dramatically, as in the summer of 1887 she was able to accompany Charles on a strenuous trip into the mountains of Colorado. A series of letters written by Myrtle from July to September, 1887 to Momsey reveal a vigorous woman in robust health. The family traveled to Colorado where Charles was co-owner, with a man by the name of Tom Williams, of the Zuni Mining Company, which had its principal office in Pueblo, Colorado. Zuni operated silver mines outside of the western Colorado of Silverton. The trip was a business trip for Charles on which his family, including his mother, accompanied him. The five Fillmores, Charles, Myrtle, Lowell, Rickert and Momsey traveled by train from Kansas City to Pueblo, Colorado, in mid-July. Charles, Myrtle and five-year-old Lowell went on to Silverton, and then took a four hour trip by horse and burro to the Zuni camp on Red Mountain, where Charles' company was mining for silver. Momsey was left behind with three-year-old Rickert in a hotel in Pueblo.

Myrtle, in a series of five letters from July 28th through September 11th to Momsey in Pueblo described life at a silver mining camp high up in the Rockies and indicated how she and Charles related to each other. The letters show that at this stage in their marriage Charles and Myrtle played the traditional husband and wife roles characteristic of late 19th century middle class Americans. He was the businessman and breadwinner and she was the home maker and mother. Like other women of the period, she had upon marriage abandoned her career, left her home, established a family and followed her husband as he pursued his business career.

Her first letter, written from Silverton, tells about the train ride and expresses the hope that Momsey and Rickert will soon be able to make the trip to Silverton. Myrtle reports they were fortunate to get a sleeper berth out of Pueblo, which made the ride much easier. Traveling with them on the train were "such mixed people," Myrtle reported. There were "Spanish, Mexicans, Chinese and white folks." Five-year-old Lowell, she said, was fascinated by what he saw out the window. "His attention was divided between prairie dogs and Indians. He saw teepees to his hearts content down among the Utes, and the Apaches in their blankets."[29]

Her next letter was written on August 7th from Zuni Camp on Red Mountain. She first described the trip up the mountain:

> Such a long hard climb to get here. I rode a horse part of the way. Charles and Lowell rode burros . . . We were four hours getting from town up here. The trail in places seemed almost perpendicular, in fact, most of the way… A train of burros came ahead of us and were loaded with provisions and tents and bedding for us . . . Our effects were packed securely in four Saratogas and born by the burros.[30]

Myrtle then described how she and her five year old son, Lowell, spent their days:

> Our habits are "early to rise." We breakfast as soon as the miners are through, which is 7 o'clock. After breakfast I make the bed and

94

straighten up the tent—then often we start out prospecting, taking our dinner with us. We take some pretty long runs. Saturday I do think we must have gone ten miles. We walked for miles right on top of mountains where we could look on each side. It is a dizzy path, but it doesn't effect Lowell or me—Charles says it makes him dizzy… It is a grand life, but a good deal of hard work in it, for every place is either up or down.[31]

She wrote an addendum to the letter on August 8th. Her comments give an idea of the size of the mining operation and its value.

We took a little run over to one of our prospects about a mile up yesterday. Lowell stayed with Mr. Williams and watched them pack the train of burros with minerals. There were thirty in the train. They will load another train today. The mine is immense—the new extension is the largest ore body in this country. A man came yesterday and offered them $75,000 for it, but Charles says he wouldn't take that for his own share.[32]

In Myrtle's next letter, written August 19th, she tells Momsey how much she misses Rick and expresses the hope that the two of them can come to Silverton. She acknowledged that their coming will depend on how Charles feels about it. She told Momsey that making a trip with Rickert to Zuni camp was out of the question. "I don't know what Charles will decide about your going to Silverton," she wrote. "It would scare you half to death getting up here." She then makes a comment which indicated she had recovered from the tuberculosis that threatened her life in 1885 and 1886. She wrote, "The climate is delightful tho, and its beautiful after you get here, but it is all up and down—no straight walking. I'm getting used to it, and it seems to agree with me. I was never so well."[33]

Myrtle indicated she did treatment work for a friend of Momsey's while in the mountain. She told Momsey, "I treated Lavinia for nearly a week after your request. If it does her any good, will be glad to continue." She then made a comment which indicated that at this point in their marriage Charles was the dominant partner. She wrote, "Hope I can see Mrs. Small (a Colorado woman who became a regular correspondent and life-long friend) when I go back. Expect Charles will go with such a rush that he won't let me see anyone." She closed by indicating how much she missed Rick. "Rick's mamma," she wrote, "wants to stop climbing mountains and hug and kiss him ever so bad."[34]

Only one letter from Momsey to the family at Zuni camp survives, that written on August 25th. It contains news about Rick and tells of her decision to remain in Pueblo rather than make the trip to Silverton.[35] Myrtle's last surviving letter to Momsey was written on September 11th. Winter was already setting in the mountains. "We have already had two snows," she reported. Her thoughts were on returning to Kansas City. "If it should turn snowy and stormy, I should feel like starting back." Charles apparently had other ideas. Myrtle told Momsey, "I expect you will be looking for us this week, but I fear we shall disappoint you. Charles is making arrangements for another month's work, and I dislike to leave him too long." Charles wanted to stay because of the prospects of striking rich silver ore. She explained,

> There seems a fair prospect of striking high grade ore in the tunnel now, which when done will give work that will pay. There are some claims we have located, Charles wants to get it worked. One we have named "The Rick," and would you believe it, the top outside rock assays 1 lb. of silver—that promises a rich mine when we get in.[36]

Myrtle wrote a brief addendum to the letter dated September 12th. Charles was about to leave for Silverton and would take the letter. Again, the weather was on her mind, as it was snowing. She reported:

> It is a grand sight to see the storms come boiling up the mountains—you hear the roar… Still there is no danger in any of these mountain storms—with half the threatening, we would be scared to death in Missouri.[37]

Given the four hour trip to Silverton, and the bad weather, it was unlikely that Charles would make it back to Zuni camp that evening. Though she did not feel there was any danger, she was not looking forward to spending the night without him:

> I expect Charles will not be back tonight—he has only stayed away one night before—I feel a strange loneliness when he is gone, tho of course there is no danger—we are near the cabin where 6 or 8 men sleep.[38]

There is no information on when they returned to Kansas City, though Myrtle expressed the hope that it would be before October 1st, 1887.

# ❧ 8 ❧
## Family

F amily was extremely important to Myrtle. Married at age 36, which was late for a woman of her era; she was 44 when her third child was born. Charles, her three sons and her mother-in-law were the five most important people in her life. In addition, she carried on an active correspondence throughout her lifetime with her siblings as well as with nephews, nieces and cousins. Much of what we know about her family life was contained in letters to family members who lived outside Kansas City.

### Grandmother Fillmore (Momsey)

Throughout her marriage to Charles, Myrtle remained close to her mother-in-law, Mary G. Fillmore. Myrtle's affection for "Momsey," as Grandmother Fillmore was affectionately called, was shown in the long letters that Myrtle wrote to her in the summer of 1887 from Silverton, Colorado. The tone of the letters is much more that of a friend than of an in-law. Their closeness in age—Momsey was only 11 years older than Myrtle—probably made friendship easier. Each of the existing letters Myrtle wrote to Momsey expressed a warmth of feeling that apparently continued throughout their lifetime—forty years of which they lived in the same house in Kansas City.

Momsey provided a valuable service for the family, not the least of which was freeing Myrtle to pursue Unity work. Lowell recalled, "My grandmother helped care for my brother and me and did the cooking for the family,"[1] She was an excellent cook, transforming the simplest foods into the most delicious dishes.[2]

Momsey lived with Charles and Myrtle in their house on Wabash Street in Kansas City until the early 1920s when a wood frame farm house at Unity Farm was remodeled for her. Charles and Myrtle moved from the Wabash street house shortly after Momsey left, occupying two residences, one at Unity Farm next door to Grandma's house, called "The Arches." The other was an apartment in town to the rear of Unity headquarters on Tracy Avenue. During the last years of Momsey's life, when she was in her nineties, the family's social activity revolved around her household.

Resilient as she was, during the last decade of her life Momsey had her ups and downs health-wise. She could also be difficult. Myrtle reflected on her foibles in a letter to her sister in 1925. She wrote:

Grandmother's condition seems just now the only cloud at the Farm. She has gone back to almost her first condition. We have to have a nurse for her, and then she wants some of us with her too. It is very hard for one to stay long where she is. She moans continually. I asked her why—and she answered, that something seemed to catch down there, and it eased her to make that sound. Well, I notice when you are telling her anything to get her interest, the moaning ceases, and while you have her interest. She can really get about, herself, most of the time—but nights are her worst time. She still keeps tabs on what's being done about the house and you hear from her when anything goes wrong. She says she can't feel the silent treatment any more… Dr. Marie says it is in her heart, and is giving her heart-tonic for heart action.[3]

The medical doctor Myrtle referred to was Dr. Marie Esmond of Kansas City. In all probability the doctor was called because Momsey wanted her. It is doubtful that Myrtle, on her own accord, would have summoned a medical doctor. Myrtle then made a poignant observation, indicating in part why Dr. Marie was called, and suggesting that, despite the years of exposure to Unity teachings, Momsey never fully accepted them. She wrote

Well, I am sure it is not for lack of opportunity that Mary Fillmore is still wandering in the darkness—her son Charles is a great light—but I've often wondered how he ever happened into her family.[4]

Myrtle indicated she had tried her best to instill Unity principles in her mother-in-law, and would continue her efforts. Nevertheless, she ends the letter with a note of resignation:

Well, spiritual things must be spiritually discerned. I've done my best, I know, to help her into spiritual understanding—and am still praying—Let there be light for this dear Soul.[5]

Grandmother Fillmore died in her home at Unity Farm on the morning of March 12th, 1931 at age ninety-seven.

The death certificate was signed by the same Dr. Marie Esmond who had previously attended her. Dr. Esmond was not at her bedside when she passed, and saw her last on February 3rd. She listed the cause of death as "Anemic endocarditis deficiency" with senility as a contributing cause.[6] Despite Grandma Fillmore's advanced age and weakened physical condition, Myrtle believed that if her mother-in-law had fully understood and applied Truth Principles she would have regained her health and continued living. Myrtle expressed this opinion to several people. To her cousin "Lottie" she asserted:

> Her wonderful vitality would have carried her through, if she had only trusted it and caught the consciousness of its eternal existence in the Father-Life. "Not by (personal) might, nor by (personal) power, but by my Spirit, saith Jehovah of hosts." If only she could have realized this great truth.

Considering her commitment to the welfare of children, her work as a school teacher for over a decade, her concerns about "Harmony in the Home" and her deep interest in motherhood, it is not surprising that Myrtle was a loving mother to her three sons. She developed a close bond with all three—Lowell, Rickert and Royal. The fact that each of them followed her into Unity work was a tribute to the example she set.

## Lowell

Born in Pueblo, Colorado on January 4, 1882, Lowell Fillmore was involved in Unity work from an early age.[8] "I must have been ten years old when I first went to work in Unity," he recalled. "On Saturdays when there was no school I would go down to the office, or as we called them, the 'Unity Rooms,' and there I would wrap for mailing the magazines that my father and mother were publishing." His mother, who began editing Wee Wisdom magazine in 1893, involved her eleven-year-old son in important ways. She often asked his opinion on articles she was publishing for her reading audience of elementary-school-age children. Lowell's home life during his boyhood was apparently a happy one. In later years he remarked, "I believe it can be truly said that my boyhood home was a household of faith."

After completing high school in 1899 Lowell, unlike his two younger brothers, did not seek a college education. Instead, he went to work for the Unity Tract Society, embarking on a career that would last sixty-four years. At the outset he performed a variety of menial chores around the office. In 1907 the business manager, Charles Prather, resigned, and Lowell took over his duties.

Lowell was also active in the local Unity Society of Practical Christianity, the church organization that held services on Sundays as well as meetings during the middle of the week. In addition to attending Sunday services,, Lowell taught Sunday school, beginning as a teen-ager when the boys in his classes were almost his age. When the first Unity youth group, the "Joyful Circle," was organized in the early 1900s, Lowell was one of the first members. He participated for many years.

In May 1909 Lowell became editor of a small weekly paper that the local Unity Society established to help its members keep in close touch with all phases of the work. Called *Weekly Unity*, its initial purpose was to publish news items along with a schedule of meetings and reports on the society's business. Intended for local distribution only, its original mission did not include an outreach to Unity readers outside of Kansas City. It was later expanded to include readers from the United States and abroad, and became one of Unity's most widely read publications.

With the incorporation of the Unity School of Christianity in 1914, Lowell, then thirty-two, became the school's general manager. It was Lowell's job to manage the school and its expanding publications program. He took over as head of Unity School in 1933 when his father, then seventy-nine, withdrew from day-to-day involvement. With his father's death in 1938, he became president of Unity School, a position he held until 1964 when he became president emeritus. He remained active until his death in 1975.

Lowell probably did more to popularize the Unity teachings than either of his parents. The audience he attracted during his sixty years as editor of Weekly Unity magazine and as author of the column "Things to be Remembered" was much wider than the audience his father attracted through his books and articles or the audience Myrtle attracted through her letters and articles. Lowell's popularity was in large part due to the clarity with which he presented the Unity spiritual teachings. He had the ability to make them understandable to people who were being exposed to them for the first time.

Lowell played a key role in the growth of the Unity movement. He originated the Prosperity Bank plan, which was responsible for Unity's vast growth from 1910 to 1950.

## Rickert

Except for a short time working as an independent architect, Rickert worked in the movement until his death at age 81.[9] Two years younger than his brother Lowell, Waldo Rickert Fillmore was born in Pueblo, Colorado on June 1, 1884. He was the second Fillmore son to be named after a famed American Transcendentalist. Lowell was the namesake of James Russell Lowell, and Rickert was named after Ralph Waldo Emerson.

Family life throughout Rickert's youth was centered around Unity work. Free time from school was often spent running errands at the offices of the Unity Tract Society. His talents as an artist surfaced early, and his mother involved him as a teenager in drawing illustrations for *Wee Wisdom* magazine. Growing up, he was particularly close to his mother. While in high school he wrote a piece for *Wee Wisdom* entitled "The Evolution of Santa Clause." It was a clearly written and carefully constructed piece that contained some unusual insights for a young man of seventeen. It seemed to reveal Rick as a promising young writer. It was not until the next issue of the magazine appeared that the editor, his mother, notified readers that she had rewritten the piece before publication, and that her son was deeply offended by the changes. He wanted it know "that he wasn't going to own the story at all, and wasn't going to write for anybody that meddled with his stories."

Rickert's response was the first public display of a strong, independent, self-believing, self-assertive personality—traits he exhibited throughout his lifetime. Not drawn to writing and teaching like his father and mother, he pursued the world of art after finishing high school in 1901. He enrolled in the Chicago Art Institute, spending four years studying there. Returning to Kansas City, he worked as an illustrator and graphic designer for several years before leaving in 1910 for a six-month tour of Europe, studying art for a time in Rome. His education and travel provided him with a more cosmopolitan outlook than his older brother, Lowell.

In 1919 when Unity School was in a rapid phase of expansion, Charles Fillmore and his sons began looking for a new site for Unity headquarters. Space for expansion at 917 Tracy Avenue in Kansas City was limited. It also seemed that the inner-city environment would not serve the long-term needs of the movement. They began looking in rural areas outside Kansas City for more suitable property. In 1919, land was selected seventeen miles southeast of Kansas City near the little village of Lee's Summit, and in 1920 it was purchased.

Rickert, though he had no architectural or engineering training, was authorized by his father to begin planning and designing the first buildings. When he was a student in Rome he had learned to love buildings in the Italian Renaissance style. He decided to copy that style along with the English Cotswold design in the construction of buildings on the new property. He immediately began landscaping and designing the Unity Tower and the Silent Unity building, which were completed in 1929, cooperating with architects Elmer Boillot and Jesse Lauck. He also constructed recreational facilities for Unity workers (tennis courts, a golf course, and a swimming pool), and operated a farm.

While Rickert was involved in planning, building and operating Unity farm during the 1920s, he was also active in community affairs. He joined the Rotary in 1924 and was active in it all his life. He served as president of the Kansas City club in 1927 and 1928 and was district governor in 1929 and 1930. While he was active in the Kansas City community, his major interest in life was building Unity Village, and making it available as a spiritual center. What he wanted more than anything else, said Dorothy Pierson, a long-time Unity minister and a friend, "was to bring people to the village, whether for education or the sharing of a wonderful atmosphere… He had a real feeling for that ground, believing his family was spiritually directed to it. He saw it as a hallowed place."

## Royal

A major sorrow in Myrtle's life was the death of her youngest son, Royal, at age twenty-five. She had involved him in *Wee Wisdom* magazine as a child, and, after graduating from the University of Missouri in 1912, Myrtle put him on the staff of the magazine as Managing Editor, a position he held until his death in 1923. Royal was the only one of her three sons whom she worked closely with professionally.

On August 6th, 1921, Myrtle's 76th birthday, Royal was in the East with his pregnant wife Frances Sleater Fillmore. He wrote these lines of appreciation of his mother in the form of a poem:

*To my beloved Mother—who bore me*
*nurtured me through my forming days;*
*befriended me in my growing days;*
*prayed for me in my stress and storm;*
*guided me wisely in mating season;*
*and rejoices with me in my approaching parenthood;*
*God bless my wonderful Mother.*[10]

Frances died in late 1921 shortly after giving birth to a daughter, who was named Frances after her mother. Myrtle felt it was a blow that Royal never fully recovered from. Weight was an issue for Royal. He was always big, weighing as much as 260 pounds, suffered from high blood pressure, and was in ill-health for about two years prior to his death.[11] He died on September 9, 1923, shortly after to going to Battle Creek, Michigan to become a patient in the Battle Creek

102

Sanitarium, get medical treatment, some needed rest and eat health foods.[12] Upon his arrival at the sanitarium he was examined by medical doctors and informed that his blood pressure was 216-180.[13] The doctors recommended medication, but Royal refused. He reported to his parents in a letter written later that day:

> **They examined me this morning and told me a lot of dope, and wanted to give me some stuff to keep my heart boosted, 'digitalis' I think it was. I told them I didn't take drugs.[14]**

The doctors persisted, but Royal did not believe that drugs would help him, believing that the best chance for his survival lay in practicing Unity Principles. "They said all right and tried to scare me up a bit," Royal wrote. "They did what I thought they would and just put me to bed for a while." Royal then began a program of fasting and prayer which lasted until he died the following Sunday morning. "I'm fasting now so please treat me for strength and wisdom," he wrote to his parents.[15]

His friend, A.M. Colby, accompanied him to Battle Creek, informed the Fillmores by telegram of Royal's death. "Royal passed away very suddenly at seven o'clock this morning he simply went to sleep in his chair. There was no suffering."[16] More details of Royal's passing were provided in a letter written from Unity headquarters to the Sleater's, Royal's in-laws. The writer stated:

> **Colby, who shared a room there with Royal, tells us that Saturday night Royal experienced great difficulty in breathing, and early Sunday morning got quite comfortable sitting in a large easy chair. About seven o'clock Sunday morning he went quietly to sleep. On Thursday evening before, he had an experience of difficulty in breathing, but he rallied and seemed so much better toward the end of the week, and Mr. Colby was greatly shocked at his going.[17] The death certificate listed the cause of death as "chronic interstitial nephritis" (inflammation of the kidneys) and "myocarditis" (inflammation of the muscular walls of the heart), the duration of these illnesses—two years.[18]**

Myrtle's reaction to her son's passing was expressed in letters to her sister and to a friend. Myrtle does not mention any physical illnesses that might have contributed to his death. She expressed the depth of feeling she had for her lost son. She wrote:

Things are adjusting themselves. Rick is trying to fill the place—the big place—Royal's going has left. Dear boy! Everybody misses him, he was so wonderfully responsive. There didn't seem a thing in any department that he could not lend a hand to help out on. His clear sightedness and sympathy were great factors in the work. … Well, I am thankful that his record here was in keeping with it, great Soul, and I am sure he is not idle wherever he is. I am a grateful mother. All my sons are treasures. Dear Royal is still among them… I am very well and am adjusting myself though it's awful hard to let go. Royal was my girl.[19]

## Grandchildren

Myrtle did not become a grandmother until the last decade of her life. All three of her sons were over thirty when they married. Rick and Harriet had two children, Charles Rickert, born in 1921 and Rosemary in 1925. Royal's daughter Frances was born in 1921. Lowell and his wife Alice bore no children, but raised Royal's daughter Frances from the age of five. All three grandchildren lived at Unity Farm. Myrtle spent time with them when she was there on weekends. Her letters were filled with news about them, the kind of comments a loving grandmother might make. "Our children are growing so nicely and play so happily out at the Farm," she wrote to a friend in 1927. "The two older children, Charles Rickert and Frances, are going to school in Lee's Summit and are making good grades."[20]

Two of her three grandchildren played significant roles during the latter half of the twentieth century in the work of the Unity School of Christianity. They were Charles R. Fillmore and Rosemary Fillmore Rhea.

## Charles R. Fillmore

The son of Rickert and Harriet Fillmore, Charles R. was born in 1921 and grew up at Unity Farm.[21] Charles R. who was ten when his grandmother died, viewed his grandmother as a teacher and disciplinarian. "When she was around we needed to mind our manners," he recalled. His grandfather Charles was more playful, less serious and less concerned about decorum. "We could yell and scream and fight," he said, around his grandfather, but not around Myrtle.

Though from a family deeply immersed in Unity teaching, he was not instructed by his parents. "Listen to what Papa Charley says," his father told him, when the subject of religion came up. This was not an easy task, since the boy did not understand much of what his grandfather had to say. It was in Sunday school that he learned the Unity teaching.

Charles R. attended elementary and high school in what was then the small town of Lee's Summit, graduated with a degree in journalism from the University of Missouri in 1943, married his high school sweetheart Anne Jones, received a commission in the U.S. Navy, and served as an executive officer aboard a minesweeper in World War II.

He returned at war's end, and in 1946 began working for Unity School. Since his grandparents, father and two uncles had devoted their lives to Unity, it was undoubtedly expected that he would follow in his family's footsteps. His first assignment was a comedown from the responsibilities he had held in the Navy. He was put to work cleaning the printing presses and sacking mail. During his first decade as a Unity employee, he worked in every department in the school.

Charles R. credits May Rowland, director of Silent Unity and member of the Unity board of trustees, with pushing him ahead and enabling him to prepare for his future role as president of Unity School. It seems that in the 1950s neither his father, Rickert, nor his uncle Lowell, both in their seventies, were concerned about moving him up and giving him the necessary experience to serve as the school's president. He was in line for the presidency because of the legal structure of Unity School. The school, though granted non-profit status by the IRS in 1926, had a unique corporate charter. Organized under the Corporation Law of Missouri in 1914, a majority of the school's fifty shares of stock were held by members of the Fillmore family. While ownership of the stock did not entitled them to receive dividends, majority ownership did authorize the family to operate the business tax-free. Charles R., the only male in the third generation of Fillmores, was the logical choice to become majority stockholder and take over management of the school at the retirement of his uncle and his father.

May Rowland, whom Charles R. viewed as a guiding spirit of the Unity work and a power behind the scenes, prodded both his father and uncle to take steps to prepare him for his future role. She told them: "Charles needs to be directed in the work," and urged that he be enrolled in the Unity Training School's ministerial education program. They complied and Charles R. matriculated and graduated. Although he had no desire to be ordained or serve in a ministerial capacity, the program, he reported, "opened new vistas" for him.

In 1955 he was appointed public relations director of Unity School, and in

1963 he became executive vice president and chief operating officer. In 1971, shortly before the death of Lowell Fillmore, he became president and chairman of the board of trustees. He served as president until 1987. Charles R never considered himself to be a spiritual teacher or leader, and was not the kind of person who called attention to himself. In an interview published in The Kansas City Star in 1979, he explained: "I'm not the spiritual leader of Unity. I'm much more a custodian, a steward. In a more recent interview, he conveyed the same message. He viewed himself as a "caretaker," as one who saw his role as "carrying out the philosophy, goals, and wishes of the founders and preserving the Unity teaching as presented by them."

Charles R.'s major contribution to Unity has been through strong administrative and financial management. James Dillet Freeman, one Unity's most highly respected spiritual teachers, who worked closely with Charles R. for several decades, characterized him as "a damn good businessman, intelligent and totally committed to Unity." William B. Dale, a member of the Unity School board of trustees, found him to be "bright, shrewd, interested, committed to the work, and a good delegator of authority. Unity School prospered during the years of Charles R's presidency—he kept the organization operating on a financially sound basis throughout his tenure in office. Operational surpluses were used to purchase adjoining farm land and to construct new buildings on the Unity campus.

### Rosemary Fillmore Rhea

The granddaughter of Charles and Myrtle Fillmore, Rosemary was born in 1925, the daughter of W. Rickert and Harriet Collins Fillmore.[22] She grew up in Unity Village, which at the time was known as Unity Farm, and as a child was personally close to her grandfather, Charles Fillmore. Some of her fondest memories growing up were of times spent with him. She recalls in particular times when she was ill. He would come and sit beside her bed, and she would begin to feel better.

In 1947 Rosemary married Stanley Grace, a local resident, and became a wife and mother. The couple had two children, Stanley Rickert Grace, and Rosalind Fillmore Grace. In 1956, when her children were school age, she went to work for WHB, a Kansas City radio station, hosting a show called *Young Ideas*. It featured interviews with young persons concerning current events. The following year the president of WHB became president of KMBC, Channel 9 in Kansas City, and asked Rosemary to adapt Unity's *Daily Word* magazine for television. The result was a five-minute program consisting of the word for the day, a passage from the Bible, a short meditation and an inspirational thought. Presented as a nondenominational film featuring Rosemary as host, the program enjoyed a twelve-year run. At its height, it appeared on seventy-five television stations nationwide. In 1968, when the program closed, she reported: "It is the most gratifying work I ever had done… We get several hundred letters a week from all over the country, and it is most comforting to realize the messages are helpful in the daily lives of people.

In 1966, after almost twenty years of marriage, Rosemary and Stanley Grace were divorced. Two years later she married Ralph Rhea, a Unity minister who had enjoyed a long and successful career in Unity. She found Rhea to be an amazing person and her marriage to him, she reported "was everything that my first marriage wasn't." In 1969, shortly after their marriage, they began working together on a program entitled, *The Word*. Like her previous program, *The Daily Word*, it was meant to be inspirational. In an effort to make *The Word* more attractive to stations during public service time, the program was condensed from five minutes to sixty seconds and taped for distribution to area radio stations. Ralph Rhea wrote the script and Rosemary narrated. A single word used in ever day language was selected; the word was then built upon to give it new meaning.

The program's ultimate success in television was due in large part to the Rheas' ability to attract celebrities from the entertainment and sports fields to handle the broadcasts. The Rheas went to Hollywood, not knowing anyone. A chance encounter with the mother of movie star Robert Wagner, who was a Unity student, opened the door. "One star introduced us to another," Rosemary recalled. A long list of well-known people handled the broadcasts, including Steve Allen, Phyllis Diller, Anne Francis, Ernest Borginine, Phil Silvers, Jane Russell and football star Mike Garrett. In 1980, in recognition of her long work with Unity, Rosemary was granted special ordination in the Unity ministry.

In 1989, after the death of Ralph Rhea, Rosemary joined the staff of the Unity School for Religious Studies, and became an "ambassador of goodwill" for Unity. She accepted speaking engagements in Unity churches and centers around the country. She had the special ability to connect her listeners to the Unity message as she had received it form her parents and grandparents. She continued at Unity School until she retired in 1998. Since then she has spent her retirement years living at Unity Village and in Jamaica.

# ❧ 9 ❧
## *Passing*

Myrtle's death on October 6, 1931 came as no surprise to her family. While she had worked at the Unity headquarters until the day before her death, and did not appear to be in ill health, she told Charles several weeks before, as well as other members of her family and friends, that she was soon going to make her transition (transition is the term Unity uses to describe the physical death of the body). Charles, in a letter to a close personal friend of Myrtle's, shortly after her death, indicated that Myrtle had expressed her intention to pass on and could not be persuaded to reconsider. Charles said that her passing was easy, painless and by choice. Without illness or suffering she simply slipped from the world of the living into the world of spirit on the evening of Tuesday, October 6, 1931 at Unity Farm. Charles wrote:

> **Tuesday night, October 6, Mrs. Fillmore passed into a new phase of expression. She decided several weeks ago that she wished to make this change, and it was with this idea in her mind that she peacefully passed out of the body. Frequently, to those nearest and dearest, Mrs. Fillmore spoke of feeling that she was ready to make the change. It was difficult for us to share her opinion, especially since she was in very good health radiantly happy, and filled with life, energy and vitality. But nothing that we could say influenced her decision.[1]**

Charles was not the only one Myrtle told of her intention to pass on. Sometime in September she told her granddaughter, Frances, that she would not be there for her tenth birthday on October 1st, and that she would not be able to help her with her thank you notes as she had done in years past. Frances recalled, "She was not in bed, not sick, and going to the office every day, but she seemed to know that she was going on."[2]

About two weeks before she died she confided in her friend, Ernest Wilson. She came personally to see him at Unity headquarters, climbing four flights of stairs to his office. It was "a sunny, smiling visit," he remembered. Wilson described the occasion and related their conversation:

> **She came to tell me she was going to leave us. My dismay must have been obvious. She hastened to explain. She was tired. She had gone on for some forty five years… She wanted to make a change. She was**

going to relinquish her physical body and go into the next dimension.

"But you can't do this to us, Mrs. Fillmore," I protested. "We need you. Mr. Fillmore may be the mind of Unity, but you're the heart. We need the heart as well as the mind."

"Now Ernest, you know better. It's time for me to make the change. Besides, you know I can help more from the other side of life than I can from this." We had an affectionate exchange of farewells. She greeted the members of the staff as usual and waved another farewell by the elevator and was gone.[3]

A Silent Unity worker, a young woman, reported that Myrtle told her that she, Myrtle, heard a voice speaking to her one day at the office when she was opening the mail. It said, "God wants you to bless the mail from the next plane of life. You will be able to accomplish much more that way."[4] Myrtle also told her son Lowell that she would soon be making her transition. In a letter to H. Emilie Cady, Lowell reported their conversations:

Mother had spoken many times during the past year of wishing to make the change in her life, and two weeks before she left she mentioned it to several friends. Naturally, we tried to dissuade her. We told her how much we needed her here, how much the Unity work needed her, but she said, "How do you know I mightn't do better work from the other side?" You see, she had a vision of a greater work to be accomplished, and we, who may not fully grasp her spiritual outlook, could but withdraw our argument and stand by with thoughts of love and strength, and joy, so that her beautiful soul may have freedom in Spirit to continue its chosen work. We have loosed her, dear friend, and let her go.[5]

Her good friend Pearl Duval, who had lunch with Myrtle a few days before she died, testified to how Myrtle prepared those around her for her passing. She wrote:

On Wednesday, September 30, I came to the Center and had lunch with Myrtle Fillmore—a visit I shall never forget. I had never seen her more radiantly happy, her eyes simply sparkled. It was the next day she left her office saying she was going to make "the change." … Every phase of "the change" was made in Divine Order. She spent the day

writing letters, receiving callers, and in helping with the regular healing work at Silent Unity. I understand she went to each desk in Silent
Unity and placed a rose on the desk... Mrs. Fillmore remarked to a
friend that she wanted to make a change saying, "I believe it would
be easier for me to do the work that is ahead of me from the invisible
plane... I am a child of the King—the King commands."[6]

Tesla Landon Wallace, the 37-year-old daughter of one of Myrtle's closest
friends, testified that she and her mother visited Myrtle on the day she died.
Her brief account of the meeting indicated that Myrtle had command of her
faculties.

In October we had a call to please go out to the Village, Aunt Myrtle
wanted to see Mother and I. She looked so sweet, but she told Mother
and I that she felt she had finished her work here and could do more
on the other side. That night she passed very quietly. October 6th,
1931.[7]

An obituary of Myrtle published in *Unity* magazine indicated that Myrtle
was in good health when she made her transition, and could have continued
living had she so chosen. Her passing was a matter of her own choosing. The
obituary stated:

Myrtle Fillmore, one of the founders of Unity School of Christianity,
passed on to the invisible side of life on Tuesday, October 6. Those
who knew her intimately and to whom she had expressed a desire to
make the change believe that she might have remained in the body
indefinitely, had she so chosen.[8]

Assuming Myrtle was in good health at the time of her passing, and that she
made a painless transition, of her own choosing, how do we explain Myrtle's
abandonment of regeneration of the physical body as a primary goal for her
life? A review of Myrtle's statements on regeneration during the last twelve
months of her life reveal her continuing commitment to it. On November 10,
1930, she wrote to a Mrs. Pratt about the body's inherent resiliency. "There is
no reason why all people should not grow more healthy, happy, strong and alive
continually. God will never let His universe get in a run-down condition."[9] In
a letter on November 4, 1930, to a Mrs. Armstrong she suggested that permanent healing of the body was possible if thoughts were properly directed:

Certain thoughts produce certain conditions in the body, so we teach that man should spiritualize all his thinking, and thus find the way to permanent healing—even eternal life. The body is the fruit of the mind. "Every good tree brought forth good fruit."[10]

She told Puella Mason on December 8, 1930 that thoughts of aging and death should be erased:

All thoughts of age and decreasing vigor are now being wiped out of your mind completely, and in place of these errors, the life idea is becoming thoroughly established in your consciousness…In your Real Self you are an ageless, deathless, eternal, free Spirit. Your body will manifest the Truth of your Being just as fast as you incorporate into your body consciousness the idea of God Mind.[11]

On January 30, 1931 she gave instructions to Mrs. Maude Armstrong, who asked about Unity's teachings concerning the regeneration of the body and overcoming death:

We have consecrated our whole lives to the Jesus Christ teaching, and we believe that those who are steadfast in practicing the principles that He demonstrated, will overcome the death of the body, just as He did. One of the essentials in attaining eternal life, and in the redemption of the body, is to keep the attention *undivided and fixed upon the Life of God within us.* We cannot do this and think habitually about souls that have lost their temples of the Holy Spirit.[12]

On February 3, 1931 she told a Mrs. Flint that when we developed a Christ consciousness we would regain our youth and never lose it:

When we learn how to find the Christ in ourselves, and draw constantly upon the inner fountain of life, our youth will be renewed as the days and years go by. Time will but increase our strengths and youthfulness, because we will be under the law of the Spirit of Life in Christ Jesus, instead of under the law of sin and the "last enemy."[13]

On April 6, 1931 in a letter to a Mrs. Boardman, Myrtle told the story of how a Kansas City gypsy woman, upon reading her palm, told her she should have died long ago. Myrtle told the gypsy that it was her commitment to the Jesus Christ teaching that kept her alive. Myrtle testified

I was down town in one of our department stores purchasing some decorations for our home, when a Gypsy woman came along and showed a great deal of interest and asked to read my palm. I explained that I did not put much confidence in palmistry and such things, but I humored her and let her read whatever she saw written upon my hand. She was greatly amazed when she saw the life line and said that I had outlived my time many years, and seemingly could not understand it. I explained to her that Jesus Christ taught that "Whosoever liveth and believeth on me shall never die."[14]

On June 3, 1931 she told a Mrs. Crater that if we observe Divine Law our bodies will remain forever youthful:

There is no reason why folks shouldn't grow more youthful in appearance, to correspond with the newness of mind and spirit. All of us are going to come to the place where we will keep our bodies strong, young, vigorous in spite of the years that pass, because it is a law that the body manifests what we have established in our minds.[15]

In a letter to Mabel Low on August 14th, just one week after Myrtle's 86th birthday, she again stressed the importance of staying focused on being youthful:

The belief in old age is something we must get rid of in our understanding of Eternal Life and Youth. It does not belong to God's creation. We must keep our eyes single to the Perfect Creation.[16]

She continued on this same theme in a letter to Matilda McNemar on August 25th declaring, "So long as we are growing we are becoming younger, newer. It's only when we cease to grow and go forward that we let our minds get 'old' and crystallized."[17]

On Wednesday, September 30th, just seven days before she died, Myrtle again wrote about the conditions surrounding Grandmother Fillmore's passing. In a letter to Lucy Kellerhouse she professed her belief that Grandma Fillmore would have gone on living if she had fully believed in Truth principles:

Yes, our Grandmother Fillmore left us the 12th of last March, after living more than 97 years. She would have been 98 had she lived in her temple flesh until October. Her faculties were keen and bright until the last. During the last few months before her transition she had three nurses to take care of her physical needs, as well as all the spiritual help that could be given. If only she had fully grasped the eternal Life Principle, and been able to direct its vitalizing energies that filled her body temple to those parts that needed renewing, she would have continued to be with us.[18]

Why did Myrtle fail to undertake what she was sure her 97-year-old mother-in-law was capable of doing—that is, directing her body's "vitalizing energies… to those parts that needed renewing"? At age 86 she was nine years younger than her mother-in-law, and apparently, in much better health. For forty years Myrtle had been teaching bodily regeneration and engaging in spiritual practices aimed toward facilitating it. Why did she seemingly abandon her own teaching? It appears that sometime during the last months of her life she concluded that she would not succeed in raising her Christ consciousness to the level where her own body would be regenerated sufficiently to overcome physical death. In a series of comments to a variety of correspondents she indicated that the task might be beyond her. In a letter to Dr. Benjamin Hauser on April 22, 1930, she acknowledged that working with her mind had not stopped the aging process. She was concerned about being able to continue to function well physically, and believed her health could be improved through proper food intake. She wrote asking for help:

> After a certain amount of wear and tear, especially after we're living on "borrowed time", as the world would call the passing of the three-score and ten mark, we find ourselves worn a bit and in need of very practical help, for we have no intention of allowing ourselves to be "placed on the shelf." There will come the time when we can draw forth from the universal mind-stuff, just the elements we need in their right proportions and relation, to maintain the proper balance in our organism. We shall be able to draw chemical substances from the fourth dimension realm, down into our physical body. But in the meantime we need to make practical the knowledge we have concerning bodily renewal, through using intelligence, discrimination, in our food selection. And so I am seeking your help, and shall be more than glad for anything that you can tell me, to help along the work of bodily transformation and renewal…Perhaps with your instruction I can follow a feeding system that will be entirely satisfactory.[19]

In two revealing letters Myrtle acknowledged she lived in a way that was hard on her body. In a letter to the Lathrops in September, 1928, she reported that she pushed herself too much and it affected her health. She wrote:

> I think it may encourage you to admit that my days of quiet were not all as pleasant as they might have been. In fact, some of those first days at home were anything but quiet—I was in great distress… I am trying to be a little more considerate of my body. I have always brought it under the dominion of my mind. And no doubt it often needed relaxation and rest and the opportunity to do its work."[20]

She admitted the same downfall in a letter to Helen Mack. "I have always demanded of my body that it keep going, doing the bidding of my mind, regardless of whether it was really wisdom which prompted or only human desires and beliefs."[21]

In several letters written during the last years of her life she let others know that she had more inner work to do before she would be able to demonstrate, on a consistent bases, the Christ Consciousness. In a letter to Caroline Risley in September, 1928, she acknowledged that she lived too much in her head.

> You say you heartily wish you could manifest the spiritual consciousness that I possess so abundantly! and I want you to know that you and I are very much alike in our development! Both of us feel the yearning for more perfect realization of spirituality. Both of us have given ourselves too much to the intellectual pursuits, and have not been entirely fair to the body man, that part of the soul which needs to deal with the manifest things, "the material" if you will.[22]

In a letter to Mrs. Kent in September, 1928, she acknowledged that she was still learning how to put on the Christ mind:

> If you are like most of us, and I believe you are, you almost hourly think, or do something, or are moved by some impulse, which admits your unbelief, lack of faith, lack of assurance that God is all in all. But we have the Christ Mind, and we are all learning to use it, aren't we?[23]

In a letter to Nellie Wilcox in September, 1928, she confessed that she did not consider herself free from negative beliefs:

> You might be surprised to learn that many of us here, who are endeavoring to hear and to heed the Still Small Voice daily, at times have off

days, when we are not altogether comfortable. This matter of living and understanding the Truth is a growth in soul and in body. When one is not healed, it is because of some sort of clinging to old beliefs and imperfections or lack of some of the God qualities.[24]

When she was unable to maintain a positive outlook, which apparently happened on occasion, she sometimes asked her son, Lowell, for assistance. She told of an instance in September, 1930 when Lowell helped her gain perspective. She wrote to a friend:

I've been getting along wonderfully well, but last week I had a little overcoming to do; Lowell helped me a lot. He sat down and talked things over and we went into the silence for a while. Then the old, unhappy frame of mind let loose and is passing away, so now I am beginning to feel more like my Christ Self again.[25]

She acknowledged in 1928 that she had not yet learned how to gain permanent access to the Christ consciousness. Myrtle wrote, "We don't claim to have proved in our own lives all the Truth that we are learning and that we express in our writings."[26] She told Ella F. Helm on September 29, 1928, that she still had a long way to go. "I, too, am still a learner," she admitted. "I feel sometimes that I am only beginning to learn what one must know in order to live the life of God."[27] On September 28, 1931, just a week before she died, she told her former secretary, Sarah Quigley, that she was still working on herself. There is, she said, "something I am trying to cleanse my heart of—remembering some things that have a tang of bitterness. I am progressing but I am not an angel yet. There is really so much weeding to do before I behold the 'The Christ in you' that I am giving my own 'garden' much attention now."[28]

The written record does not reveal anything which fully explained Myrtle's reasons for giving up her long-sought goal of bodily regeneration and the overcoming of death. She undoubtedly discussed the question with Charles, as he indicated he tried to dissuade her from following through with her intention to make her transition. Nothing in Charles' personal papers reveals the contents of their conversation. Myrtle left no clues in the letters she wrote to correspondents, and the discussion she had with Ernest Wilson failed to address the question.

Since Myrtle's passing could be interpreted as an indication that Unity school was abandoning its teaching on regeneration of the body, Unity magazine addressed the question in its January, 1932, issue. In an unsigned article entitled, "The Passing of Myrtle Fillmore," an article that could not have been published without the approval of Charles, it was clearly indicated that Myrtle's passing in no way effected the teaching on bodily regeneration. It was stated:

> **In accepting this change, we do not desert the idea of overcoming death as did Jesus by quickening the body to a fourth-dimensional expression. But we are mindful that death is the last enemy to be overcome, that we take a very big step in that overcoming when we overcome the fear of death, and that there are many steps to take, many high adventures in God's glorious service, before that final overcoming.**[29]

A final question on Myrtle's passing needs to be address. What was the status of her health at the time of her death? Was she in perfectly good health on October 6, 1931, or was she suffering from a life-threatening disease? Was she, as Charles testified, "in very good health, radiantly happy, and filled with life, energy and vitality," or was she ill?[30] A reading of Myrtle's death certificate gives the impression that Myrtle was not at all well. The cause of death was listed as "chronic parenchymatous nephritis." This is an inflammation of the kidneys and the surrounding tissue. The word "chronic" indicates that the condition existed over a period of time. A contributory cause was listed as "Old Age." The death certificate was signed by Dr. Marie Esmond, who listed the time of death as 8:05 P.M., October 6, 1931.[31] Esmond, the medical doctor who treated Grandmother Fillmore before she died, was called to attend Myrtle at her home at Unity Farm sometime during the day of her death. The certificate reads, "I last saw her alive on October 6, 1931." Dr. Esmond was chosen to attend Myrtle, probably because she was known by the family. The illness diagnosed by Esmond was a serious one. Chronic Parenchymatous nephritis could easily cause death if not properly treated. Was Myrtle really that ill? What was the condition of her health during the final weeks of her life? Because Myrtle was such an avid letter-writer, and because she often told her correspondents how she was feeling, the status of her health is a matter of record.

During the month of August, 1931 Myrtle was living at "The Arches," her home at Unity Farm, and teaching and attending classes at the Unity Training School located on the farm. Though she normally wrote letters from her office in Kansas City, she was able to carry on her letter writing from the farm, and on August 11th wrote Marion Irons, a long-time correspondent, that she had been "resting." This was a term Myrtle often used in the past to indicate she wasn't feeling up to par. She acknowledged to Irons that she wasn't feeling well enough to attend all of the early morning prayer sessions of the Training School.[32] In letters to Aunt Ella on September 1st and Elizabeth Berlinghoff on September 8th, she also indicated that she had been "resting."[33] In a letter to her former secretary, Sarah Quigley, on September 11th she said she spend the previous week at the farm. "I rested a great deal," she said, "attending the training school occasionally."[34] On September 11th she told her "dear and beloved friend," Helen Mack, that she has spent the previous week at the Farm, "taking a nice rest, giving special attention to diet." Often in the past when Myrtle was not feeling well, she carefully watched her diet.[35] For example, in December, 1929, when she was ill with a head cold, she went on "Dr. Hauser's seven day cleansing." The diet required her to take fruit juices and broth "for eliminating."[36]

On Monday, September 14, 1931 she apparently had a bad day. Two days later she wrote Lola Jones, "I'm getting along pretty well with the diet, but Monday was something of an 'off' day, so I thought it best to stay at home all day."[37] She wrote to her friend, Laura Bolles, also on September 16th, telling of plans the family (Charles, Rick, Lowell and their wives and children) were making to visit the Ozark mountains in southern Missouri over the weekend. She wasn't sure she would be well enough to go. She wrote: "I'll have to wait until the last to decide whether or not I'll go…I have been on a diet during the past two weeks and it's not always an easy matter to stick to a prescribed course of eating while traveling, you see."[38] She acknowledged to Stella Paulus that she had been under the weather. "The first part of this month," she reported, "I stayed at the farm resting…I have not been at the office very much regularly."[39] Keep in mind that it was during this period of not feeling well that she began telling family and friends that she had decided to "make a change."

Myrtle made the trip to the Ozarks with the family over the weekend of September 18th to the 20th and had a wonderful time. From the time she returned from the Ozarks on September 21st until her death, fifteen days later, she makes no mention in her correspondence of being ill. She was apparently at the office regularly, as records indicate she wrote letters every work day. Her schedule was quite full. In response to a woman who wanted her and Charles to make an evening visit, she commented:

> **Monday evenings we have the board and club meetings, Wednesday evening we have the healing meetings; Tuesday and Thursday evening**

**we are at Unity Farm—and so on throughout the whole week we have regular duties to attend to.[40]**

She makes no mention in letters she wrote in September or early October of her intention to make her transition. She may have felt this information too personal to be put in writing. Surprisingly, in several letters she stated that she looked forward to continued regular contact with her correspondent in the future.[41] In the last letter she wrote, on Monday, October 5th, the day before she died, she indicated that she anticipated attending a play to be given by Unity workers at Unity farm the following Friday (October 9th).[42] Her correspondents would never have surmised that she was contemplating "making a change."

During the two weeks preceding her death she showed no outward signs of illness. How then, can we explain the cause of death as "chronic pranchymatis nephritis" as indicated by Dr. Marie Esmond on the death certificate? Consultations with six medical doctors, none of whom are connected with Unity, indicate that the medical technology required to make the diagnosis of "chronic paranchymatis nephritis" had not been developed by 1931. Even today such a diagnosis could not be made in a patient's home. The instrumentation required is available only in hospitals. These doctors believed that, because Dr. Esmond was required to come up with a cause of death that satisfied the Missouri State Board of Health, she chose a diagnosis that was plausible and satisfied the legal requirements. One doctor told me that if the diagnosis had been correct, Myrtle would have been bloated, having difficulty eliminating fluids, and in a lot of pain.[43] Dr. Esmond was probably unfamiliar with Myrtle's medical history. Given her continuing distrust of the medical profession, it is highly unlikely that Myrtle consulted Dr. Esmond at any time during her lifetime. She makes no mention of ever having been treated by her. The death certificate indicates that Dr. Esmond had no contact with Myrtle prior to the day of her death. Dr. Esmond's presence, however, raises the question of why was she called and by whom? Had Myrtle been perfectly well, suffering from no life-threatening medical symptoms, there would have been no need to call a doctor. If she had died in her sleep her death certificate might have been signed by a coroner rather than a family doctor.

A statement made by Myrtle in a letter to her sister, written in early March, 1931, just before Grandmother Fillmore's death, provides a clue to the family's reasoning. Myrtle commented that her mother-in-law was very uncomfortable "in her present physical condition." Myrtle noted that she had been restless and had kept her nurse busy during the night. "We are doing all we can," Myrtle assured her sister, "and since spiritual treatments have ceased to reach her, called in Dr. Marie—which of course doesn't bring her peace." Myrtle expressed the opinion that mental training and prayer were the best remedies for someone in Grandmother Fillmore's condition. "The training of the mind and soul counts in the long run," she asserted. "Spiritual things should be valued above all else. 'In Me ye shall find peace' is the teaching of the Christ mind."[44]

Myrtle gave the impression that, if it had been totally up to her, Dr. Marie would not have been called for Grandmother Fillmore. So, who called Dr. Marie Esmond for Myrtle on Tuesday, October 6, 1931, in the hours before her death? Probably not Myrtle. Was Dr. Esmond called because Myrtle, in the opinion of Charles and their two sons, was suffering from a life-threatening event and, as was the case with Grandmother Fillmore, "spiritual treatments have ceased to reach her"? Unless new information is uncovered in the form of testimonials by those at her bedside the evening she died, we will never know the answer to that question. None of the family left detailed accounts of what took place during the final hours of Myrtle's life.

Whatever the circumstances of the last hours of her life, Myrtle orchestrated the events of her passing in a remarkable way. She let family and friends know she wanted to "make a change", allowing them to get ready for it. She correctly intuited that her time of leaving was fast approaching. The testimony that she died "peacefully" probably meant painlessly, as well. Unlike many people who spend years in pain and suffering in nursing homes and hospitals waiting to die, Myrtle, despite advancing years, was in full command of her faculties. She lived a normal life right up to the end, and died in the privacy of her own home.

# *Photo Gallery*

**Left:** Family photograph, about 1910, with Charles, Momsey, Lowell (top left), Rickert and Royal. (Courtesy of Unity School Archives)

**Below:** Myrtle (third from left) and Charles with members of the Kansas City Unity Society of Practical Christianity after a Sunday morning service, about 1910. (Courtesy of the Unity School Archives)

**Left:** Myrtle with her three sons, Royal, Lowell and Rickert, about 1900. (Courtesy of the Unity School Archives)

121

**Above:** Unity headquarters, 913 Tracy Avenue, Kansas City, Missouri, about 1920. (Courtesy of the Unity School Archives)

**Right:** Myrtle as a young woman. (Courtesy of the Unity School Archives)

**Below:** The letter-writer and counselor at her desk at Unity headquarters, in the 1920s. (Courtesy of Unity School Archives)

# Notes

(The letters indicated below can be found in the Myrtle Fillmore collection, Unity Archives, Unity School of Christianity, Unity Village, Missouri)

## 1. Portrait in Sepia

1. Unity on line at *www.unity.org* "About Silent Unity."
2. *How to let God Help You*, pp. 92-93.
3. Ibid., p. 93.
4. Letter to Grace Norton August 9, 1928.
5. Letter to E. F. Helm, Date not available.
5. Gale, October 3, 1930.
6. Fillmore, Myrtle, "How I Found Health." *Unity*, August 1899, p. 68.
7. Letter to Jean, July 31, 1931. Myrtle Fillmore Collection, Unity Archives.
8. Letter to Jennie Koerner, citation not available.
9. Fillmore, Myrtle Healing Letters. Unity School of Christianity. No date listed. P. 7-8.
10. Unidentified young person.
11. Elizabeth Nov 4, 1930.
12. Elizabeth Griffith, March 19, 1929.
13. Mrs. Kent, Sept 22, 1928
14. Florence Edwards, August 7, 1931.
15. Marion Irons, October 25, 1928.
16. Her sister, D'Andrade, pp. 97-98.
17. Mrs. Kent, Sept 22, 1928.
18. Martha Smock. *Liberated Woman*, p. 4.
19. Freeman Papers, Statement of a person who attended Sunday services at the Society of Practical Christianity in Kansas.
20. Smock p. 4.
21. Donna Smythe, May 22, 1931.
22. May Rowland Papers, Unpublished manuscript, Unity Archives.

## 2. Spiritual Teaching

1. Letter to Mrs. Grater, January 14, 1930.
2. Letter to Mrs. King, December 5, 1929.
3. Letter to Jean Wilson, August 28, 1930.
4. Letter to Mrs. Spruce, March 19, 1930.
5. Letter to Madie, June 11, 1930.

### The Nature of God

1. Letter to Blanch Lewellyn, February 19, 1930.
2. Letter to Mr. Anderson, April 9, 1929.
3. Letter to Ellen Joby, June 25, 1929.
4. Letter to Caroline Risley, September 19, 1928.
5. Letter to Flora Plumstead, March 6, 1928.
6. Letter to Jeleta Clinton, March 15, 1928.
7. Letter to Mrs. Anderson, April 9, 1929.

8. Citation not available.
9. Letter to Alice Gleason, November 28,1930.

### Mind and Consciousness
1. Letter to Syarlic, February 6, 1929.
2. Letter to Mrs. Lathrop, Date not recorded.
3. Letter to Eva Stafford, August 21, 1929.
4. Letter to Helen Scott, November 8, 1929.
5. Letter to Addie Hock, July 19, 1929.

### Jesus, Christ Consciousness and Traditional Christianity
1. Letter to Elizabeth Griffiths, January 13, 1931.
2. Letter to Kate Heffelfinger, September 17, 1931.
3. Letter to Rowena, July 31, 1928.
4. Letter to Mrs. Shutts, November 14, 1930.
5. Letter to Floyd Kelly, June 1, 1931.
6. Letter to G.N. Hansen, August 24, 1931.
7. Letter to Lucia Vosper, April 2, 1930. Myrtle incorrectly assumes that the King James Bible, made in 1611 is an accurate translation of the original texts. There are many errors in that text. Since Myrtle's time there have been successful attempts by scholars of the Bible to translate from the ancient Hebrew and Greek texts. The result is a much more accurate version of both the New and Old Testament. Myrtle might not have made these statements had the current translations been available to her.
8. Letter to Elizabeth Berlinghoff, September 1, 1931.
9. Letter to Petranela Gunterman, April 4, 1929.
10. Letter to Madie, March 10, 1930.
11. Letter to Marion Irons, February 4, 1931.
12. Letter to Gene Eller, September 26, 1928.
13. Letter to Maude Armstrong, January 30, 1931.
14. Letter to Nellie Cox, September 7, 1928.
15. Letter to Lily Stack, April 11, 1928.
16. Letter to Elodia Gonzalez, January 3, 1930.
17. Letter to Nellie Wilcox, September 7, 1928.
18. Ibid.
19. Letter to Hazel Sage, June 29, 1931.

### The Carnal Mind, Race Consciousness and Sense Consciousness
1. Letter to Grace Kronkite, April 10, 1930.
2. Letter to Stella Paulus, April 10, 1930.
3. Letter to Gertrude Defrates, July 29, 1931.
4. Ibid.
5. Letter to Mrs. Anderson, April 9, 1929.
6. Letter to Alice Pummer, May 15, 1931.
7. Letter to Grace Durand, June 18, 1930.
8. Letter to Mrs. Ward, April 30, 1928.
9. Letter to Lucy Keller, March 17, 1930.
10. Letter to Sara Jennings, November 7, 1928. Rev. Michael Maday, Adjunct Professor at the Unity Institute, notes that Myrtle's interpretation of sense consciousness is crucial, and may not be completely understood by Unity people today.

11. Fillmore, Myrtle, *How to Let God Help You*. Selected and arranged by Warren Meyer. Unity Village: Unity Books, 1994, p. 119.
12. Letter to Mrs. Griffith, October 20, 1930.

### Spiritual Practice
1. Letter to Miss Nicolay, May 15, 1930.
2. Letter to Mrs. Griffith, October 21, 1930.
3. Citation note available.

### Using Intuition
1. Letter to Mrs. Ainsworth, June 5, 1930.
2. Letter to Elodia Gonzalez, January 3, 1930.
3. Ibid.
4. Letter to Marian Tally, April 26, 1929.
5. Letter to Mrs. Sekstrom, April 22, 1930.
6. Letter to Lily Stack, April 11, 1928.

### Disciplining the Mind
1. Letter to Mrs. Uhl, August 1, 1930.
2. Letter to Miss Nicolay, May 15, 1930. Myrtle often writes about the unconscious mind, but does not explain how we are to make use of it. Today we know that there are therapists who can help us discover the secrets of the unconscious mind and help us work with these new revelations.
3. Letter to Julia Bradley, September 30, 1929.
4. Letter to Mary Eaglehoff, June 17, 1929.

### Affirmations
1. Letter to Mrs. Kramer, June 12, 1928.
2. Letter to Bonita, February 11, 1929.
3. Letter to Mrs. Kramer, June 12, 1928.
4. Letter to Mrs. Eaglehoff, June 17, 1929.
5. Letter to Mrs. Hursey, September 26, 1930.
6. Letter to Anna Nicolay, March 20, 1930.
7. Letter to Adilai d'Irsay, July 20, 1931.

### Imagery
1. Letter to Mrs. Lathrop, December, 18, 1930.
2. Letter to Flora, December 22, 1930.
3. Lettere to Helen Mack, August 24, 1930.

### Denials
1. Letter to Ella Tabor, April 24, 1929.
2. Ibid. Michael Maday notes that there are some people in Unity who believe that in making a denial you claim that a condition or circumstance does not exist. Myrtle does not support this position, pointing out that you should admit that the condition exists, but that you deny that is has power over you.
3. Letter to Jean Wilson, January 9, 1930.
4. Letter to Louis Wardell, December 10, 1930.

### Divine Love
1. Letter to Fannie Wingate, May 6, 1931.

2. Letter to Aunt Ella, February 2, 1930.
3. Ibid.
4. Letter to Madeline Spencer, May 3, 1930.
5. Letter to Nina Free, January 1, 1930.
6. Letter to Fannie Wingate, May 6, 1930.
7. Letter to Mary Kohout, August 1, 1929.
8. Letter to Aunt Ella, February 13, 1930.
9. Letter to Fannie Wingate, May 6, 1930.
10. Letter Madeline Spencer, September 22, 1931.
11. Letter to Gale, October 3, 1930.
12. Letter to Fannie Wingate, December 9, 1930.

*Prayer*
1. Letter to Mrs. Murphy, January 21, 1931.
2. Letter to Mrs. Reams August 6, 1929.
3. Letter to Mrs. Kramer, June 12, 1928.
4. Letter to an unidentified correspondent.
5. Letter to Mrs. Lukens, November 12, 1930.
6. Letter to Madie, May 10, 1928.
7. Letter to J. Hutts, November 14, 1930.
8. Letter to Anna Nicolay, August 8, 1929.
9. Letter to Valorie Padelford, August 20, 1930.
10. Letter to Mollie Feldhammer, August 20, 1930.

*Meditation*
1. Letter to Clara Joseph, November 8, 1929.
2. Letter to Dr. Williams, March 11, 1931.
3. Letter to Mrs. Unger, June 13, 1928.
4. Letter to Lady Novina, Date not available.
5. Letter to Mrs. Billings, July 28, 1929.
6. Letter to Ella Richards, January 5, 1930.
7. Letter to Pella Mason, April 3, 1931.
8. Letter to Dr. Williams, March 11, 1931.

*Focusing on the present moment*
1. Letter to Gary Lidecker, May 26, 1928.
2. Letter to Willis Scott, February 8, 1931.
3. Letter to Mrs. Coons, August 12, 1929; to A. Nicolay August 8, 1929.
4. Letter to Marie Bella Irwin, May 17, 1928.
5. Letter Mrs. Wood, July 25, 1929.
6. Ibid.
7. Letter to Mrs. Lothrop, January 13, 1929.
8. Letter to Mrs. Wood, July 25, 1929.

*Joy*
1. Letter to Mary Eaglehoff, June 17, 1929.
2. Letter to Mrs. Kramer, June 20, 1929.
3. Letter to Madeline Spencer, May 3, 1930.
4. Letter to Ruth Dalrymple, June 14, 1929.

### Spiritual messages in dreams
1. Letter to L.Z. July 11, 1928
2. Letter to Stella Paulus, October 6, 1930.
3. Letter to Helen, July 16, 1929.
4. Ibid.

### Persistence
1. Letter to the Berlinghoffs, March 2, 1929.
2. Letter to the Wallaces, October 2, 1929.
3. Letter to William Green February 23, 1928.
4. Letter to Flora Reeder, August 9, 1929.
5. Letter to William Green, February 23, 1928.

### Faith
1. Letter to Elizabeth Berlinghoff, June 26, 1928.
2. Letter to Elizabeth, May 2, 1928.
3. Letter to Puella Mason, January 9, 1930.
4. Letter to Sunny Jim, May 1, 1930.
5. Letter to Puella Mason, February 2, 1931.
6. Letter to Anna Nicolay, August 8, 1929.
7. Letter to Mrs. Smallwood, July 7, 1931.
8. Letter to Thomas Newel, January 14, 1930.

### Divine Law
1. Letter to Madie, June 11, 1930.
2. Letter to Ed Hursey, August 7, 1931.
3. Letters to A.C. Norton, August 9, 1928; Harriet McDonald, August 4, 1931; Sunny Jim, May 9, 1928; Madie, January 8, 1931; Mrs. Lukens, November 13, 1930; Mrs. Platt, November 10, 1930; Fannie Wingate, December 9, 1930; Ed Hursey, August 7, 1931.

### Twelve Powers
1. Letter to Helen Glass, date not available.
2. Letter to Earl September 24, 1928. Probably the most complete presentation of how to bring the Twelve Powers into full expression is contained in *Christ Enthroned in Man*, a book written by Cora Fillmore, Charles' second wife. This book was published in 1937 at the encouragement of Charles. The "Foreword" to that book stated, "These exercises are supplementary to Charles Fillmore's book The Twelve Powers of Man, and instruct the readers of that book how to apply the principles therein laid down, and how to awaken within the body, through the action of mind, the undeveloped or sleeping faculties."
3. Letter to Jennie Koerner, December 3, 1929. The writings of Charles in *The Twelve Powers of Man* and Cora Fillmore's in *Christ Enthroned in Man* were brought together in 1998 by then editor of Unity Books, Michael Maday, in a book entitled *The Twelve Powers*. The writings of Charles and Cora on the Twelve Powers were originally published in *Unity* magazine in 1925 and 1929. The 1998 book *The Twelve Powers* brings these writings together for the first time in book form.
4. Letter to Flora Reeder, Date not available.
5. Letter to Gene Eller, September 26, 1928.
6. Letter to William Green, February 23, 1928.

### Bodily Regeneration
1. Letter to Maude Armstrong, January 31, 1930.
2. Letter to Mrs. Flint, February 3, 1931.
3. Letter to Mrs. Hazelhurst, March 21, 1930.
4. Letter to Arthur Tilton Steele, February 25, 1930.
5. Letter to M. Boardman, April 6, 1931.
6. Letter to Mrs. Hazelhurst, March 21, 1930. Myrtle and Charles's assertions regarding bodily regeneration, immortality and sexuality are not a part of the teachings of the Unity School of Christianity today.
7. Letter to Mrs. Platt, August 15, 1930.
8. Letter to Mrs. Hazelhurst, March 21, 1930.
9. Letter to Maude Armstrong, January 31, 1930.

### Reincarnation
1. Letter to Maude Armstrong, May 8, 1929.
2. Letter to Aunt Ella, February 13, 1930.
3. Letter to Mary Eaglehoff, May 26, 1928.
4. Letter to Fannie Wingate, December 9, 1930.
5. Letter to Flora Plumstead, March, (day not available) 1928.
6. Ibid.

### Influences
1. *Modern Thought*, April, 1889, p. 8.
2. *Thought*, November, 1891, p. 303.
3. Charles S. Braden, *Spirits in Rebellion: The Rise and Development of New Thought*. (Dallas: Southern Methodist University Press, 1963), p. 126.
4. *Modern Thought*, November, 1889, p. 12.
5. Witherspoon, Thomas E. *Myrtle Fillmore: Mother of Unity*. Unity Books, Unity Village, Missouri, p. 45.

## 3. Practitioner of Spiritual Healing
1. Fillmore, Myrtle, *Healing Letters*. Unity School of Christianity, No date listed, pp. 7-8.
2. Fillmore, Myrtle, "Health in the Home," *Unity*, October, 1911.
3. Ibid.
4. Letter to Mrs. Lathrop, August 15, 1928. Myrtle Fillmore collection, Unity Archives.
5. Fillmore, Lowell, "They Made a Contract with God," printed in *Guideposts*, September, 1948. Lowell Fillmore collection, Unity Archives.
6. Letters to Mrs. Zimmer, June 20, 1929 and to Jessie King, June 4, 1929, Myrtle Fillmore collection, Unity Archives.
7. Letter to Helen Brown, February 25, 1928. Myrtle Fillmore collection, Unity Archives.
8. Letter to Miss Billings, July 25, 1928, Myrtle Fillmore collection, Unity Archives.
9. Duval, Pearl. "Myrtle Fillmore," *Current Events Groups*, March 16, 1937. Pearl Duvall collection, Unpublished manuscript. Unity Archives.
10. Statement of Tesla Wallace Landon. Unpublished report, Myrtle Fillmore collection, personal file. Unity Archives.
11. Fillmore, Myrtle "Health in the Home," Op. cit.
12. Fillmore, Myrtle, *How to Let God Help You*. (selected and arranged by Warren Meyer) Unity School of Christianity. 1957, p. 178-186.
13. Ibid.

14. A copy of this placard is in the Charles Fillmore collection, Administration: Society of Silent Unity file, Unity Archives.
15. *Unity*, March 15, 1896. Unity Archives.
16. "Learning Divine Law," *Weekly Unity*, August 18, 1923.
17. Gatlin, Dana. *The Story of Unity's Fifty Golden Years*. Unity School of Christianity, 1939, p. 8.
18. *Unity*, February, 1908, Unity Archives.
19. Letter to St. Lawrence, March 22, 1930. Myrtle Fillmore collection, Unity Archives.
20. *Weekly Unity*, August 18, 1923. "Learning Divine Law." Included in this articles was a brief account of the origins of Unity work given by Myrtle Fillmore at one of the noon silences of the Unity Conference and Healing Revival, held in Kansas City in August, 1923.
21. Ibid.
22. *Unity*, August, 1903, Unity Archives.
23. *Weekly Unity*, date and page not available, 1909.
24. Ibid.
25. Letter to Minnie Lee Goodbred, September 18, 1928. Myrtle Fillmore collection, Unity Archives.
26. Letter from Ila White to an unnamed correspondent, no date, but probably 1929, Myrtle Fillmore collection, Unity Archives.

## 4. Silent Unity

1. Fillmore, Myrtle. "Absent Healing," *Modern Thought*, Volume I, No. One, p. 2.
2. The Fillmores published three other magazines in the early 1890s. These magazines differed from Unity in that they were addressed to a broader reading audience. Unity magazine, in the period 1891 to 1895, was published solely to present Truth Principles to members of the Society of Silent Unity. The other three magazines, (*Modern Thought, Christian Science Thought* and *Thought*) published from 1889 to 1895, served as a platform for the Fillmores to present the developing spiritual ideas. When *Thought* was merged with *Unity* in 1895, *Unity* became the flagship magazine of the Unity movement, the primary publication for presenting the Unity teachings to a worldwide audience.
3. *Christian Science Thought*, April, 1890.
4. *Unity*, June 1894, 14.
5. *Christian Science Thought*, April, 1890, p. 9; Unity, June 1891, p. 1.
6. *Unity*, June 1891, p. 1.
7. *Unity*, August 1894, p. 216.
8. *Unity*, March 1910, p. 206.
9. *Unity*, July 1893, p. 10.
10. *Unity*, December 15, 1897, pp. 28-29.
11. *Unity*, May 1905.
12. *Unity*, September 1906, p. 217.
13. *Unity*, March 1906, p. 166.
14. *Unity*, October 1906, p. 311.
15. Ibid.
16. *Unity*, August 1908, p. 172.
17. *Unity*, January 1902, p. 37.
18. *Unity*, December 1, 1897, pp. 463-464; Unity, December 15, 1897, p. 517; *Unity*, January 1895.
19. *Unity*, December 1, 1897, pp. 463-64.

20. *Unity*, April 1907, p. 261.
21. *Unity*, February 1902, p. 37.
22. *Unity*, April 1907, p. 161.
23. Letter to Mrs. Clubb, January 23, 1929. Myrtle Fillmore Collection, Unity Archives.
24. Letter to Fannie Wingate, August 30, 1928. Myrtle Fillmore Collection, Unity Archives.
25. *Unity*, October 1911, p. 332.
26. *Weekly Unity*, February 1910, p. 336.
27. *Unity*, October 1911, p. 332.
28. *Weekly Unity*, February 1910, p. 335.
29. *Unity*, March 1915, pp. 225-227.
30. *Unity*, March 12, 192, p. 7.
31. Vahle, Neal. *The Unity Movement: Its Evolution and Spiritual Teaching*. Templeton Foundation Press, 2002, p.175.
32. Letter from Myrtle Fillmore to Mary Grater, June 16, 1930, Myrtle Fillmore collection, Unity Archives.
33. Letter from Myrtle Fillmore to Mrs. Allen, January 16, 1931, Myrtle Fillmore collection, Unity Archives.

## 5. Teacher of Truth Principles

1. *Unity*, December 1, 1897, Unity Archives.
2. Information on these classes is contained in the December 1897 and January 1898 issues of *Unity* magazine. Unity Archives.
3. Letter from Charles Fillmore to Unity School staff, August 8, 1900. Charles Fillmore collection, Unity Archives.
4. *Unity*, October 1904. Unity Archives.
5. *Unity*, January 1899. Unity Archives.
6. Ibid.
7. *Unity*, February 1899. Unity Archives.
8. Ibid.
9. *Unity*, May 1899. Unity Archives.
10. *Weekly Unity*, September 13, 1924.
11. *Weekly Unity*, September 19, 1924.
12. *Wee Wisdom*, April 1903.
13. *Wee Wisdom*, March 1902.
14. *Wee Wisdom*, April 1893.
15. *Wee Wisdom*, March 1902
16. Gatlin, Dana, Op. cit.
17. Ibid.
18. *Wee Wisdom*, June 1902.
19. *Wee Wisdom*, May 1913.
20. *Wee Wisdom*, August 1913.
21. *Wee Wisdom*, July 1915.
22. Ibid.

## 6. Charles

1. U.S. Bureau of the Census, "Inhabitants in Sauk Rapids District in the County of Benton (Minnesota)," 1850; "County of Stearns (Minnesota)," 1860; and "3rd Ward of the City of St. Cloud (Minnesota)," 1870.

2. Dana Gatlin, *The Story of Unity's Fifty Golden Years* (Kansas City, MO: Unity School of Christianity, 1939), x-xi.

3. Ibid.

4. *Unity*, September 1896, 262.

5. Charles Brodie Patterson, "Charles Fillmore: A Biographical Sketch," *Unity* (August 1902): 69.

6. Gatlin, *Fifty Golden Years*, x-xi.

7. "Unity Religion Founder Tells What It Means," unidentified New York City newspaper article (photocopy), 1934, Charles Fillmore Collection, Unity Archives.

8. Ibid.

9. Gatlin, *Fifty Golden Years*, xi.

10. *Denison (TX) Daily News*, July 11, 1880. In a piece entitled "Finds Regrets at Gold Trail End," the editor printed a letter from Charles to K. Murphy, who apparently was a resident of Denison.

11. Gatlin, *Fifty Golden Years*, xi.

12. Ibid.

13. "Not an Answer, But an Opportunity," *Unity*, February 1894, 6.

14. Ibid.

15. Gatlin, *Fifty Golden Years*, xii.

16. James Dillet Freeman, *The Story of Unity* (Unity Village, MO: Unity Books, 1978), 27.

17. Charles Fillmore, *Biographical Sketch of Charles Fillmore: A Questionnaire*, 1927, Charles Fillmore Collection, Unity Archives.

18. *Modern Thought*, April 1889, 10.

19. Ibid., 6.

20. *Modern Thought*, June 1889, 8.

21. Ibid.

22. *Unity*, December 1891, 6.

23. *Unity*, August 1891, 6.

24. *Modern Thought*, September/October 1889, 9.

25. *Modern Thought*, February 1890, 8.

26. *Christian Science Thought*, March 1891, 5–6.

27. *Modern Thought*, March 1890, 8.

28. Ibid., 9.

29. *Thought*, September 1891, 248.

30. *Unity*, June 8991, p. 2.

31. *Unity*, July 1915, p. 88; Unity, September 1917, p. 272; *Unity*, April 1923, p. 381.

32. *Unity*, January 1, 1899, p. 325.

33. *Unity*, April 1909, p. 264.

34. Figures taken from *Weekly Unity*, June 5, 1090.

35. *Unity*, November 1900, p. 366.

36. *Unity*, March 1910, p. 277.

37. *Unity*, December 1910, pp. 544-45.

38. *Unity*, December 1891, p. 1.

39. *Thought*, December 1894, p. 414.

40. *Unity*, August 1, 1896, p. 200.

41. *Unity*, June 1, 1898, p. 113; *Unity*, June 15, 1898, p. 416, 427.

42. *Unity*, July 1909, p. 29.

43. *Weekly Unity*, November 24, 1910, p. 1.

44. *Weekly Unity,* April 13, 1913, p. 5.

45. *Unity*, September 1914, p. 254.

46. *Unity*, June 1914, p. 529.

47. Testimony of unnamed person who attended the Sunday services of the Kansas City Society of Practical Christianity. James Dillet Freeman collection, Unity Archives.

48. Ibid.

49. Martha Smock, "Myrtle Fillmore: Liberated Woman." *Unity*. September, 1974. pp. 4-10.

50. Ibid.

51. Charles Brodie Patterson. "Charles Fillmore, A Biographical Sketch," Op. cit.

52. Letter from Myrtle to Charles. August 18, 1909. Charles S. Fillmore collection, Unity Archives.

53. Letter from Myrtle to Charles. August 20, 1909. Myrtle Fillmore collection, Unity Archives.

54. Letter from Charles to Myrtle. August 20, 1909. Myrtle Fillmore collection, Unity Archives.

55. Letter from Charles to Myrtle. August 22, 1909. Myrtle Fillmore collection, Unity Archives.

56. Letter to Mary Eaglehoff. November 9, 1928. Myrtle Fillmore collection, Unity Archives.

57. Letter to Granda, February 26, 1930 and Letter to Laura Bolles, July 18, 1930. Myrtle Fillmore collection, Unity Archives.

58. Letter to Mrs. Platt, April 4, 1930. Myrtle Fillmore collection, Unity Archives.

59. Letter to Stella Paulus, February 11, 1931. Myrtle Fillmore collection, Unity Archives.

60. D'Andrade, Hugh. *Charles Fillmore, The Life of the Founder of the Unity School of Christianity*. Harper & Row, 1976.

61. Letter to a friend. No date, but probably the late 1920s. Only part of the letter remains. Myrtle Fillmore collection, Unity Archives.

62. Letter to St. Lawrence, July 10, 1930. Myrtle Fillmore collection, Unity Archives.

63. Letter to Laura Bolles, July 18, 1930. Myrtle Fillmore collection, Unity Archives.

64. Letter to M.L. Hursey, September 15, 1931. Myrtle Fillmore collection, Unity Archives.

65. Letter to Elizabeth Pettinger, March 21, 1929. Myrtle Fillmore collection, Unity Archives.

66. Letter to Kate Heffelfinger, September 17, 1931. Myrtle Fillmore collection, Unity Archives.

67. Letter to Fannie Wingate, November 20, 1929 and Mrs. Oyler, Dec 31, 1929. Unity Archives.

## 7. Early Years

1. Myrtle Fillmore, *How to Let God Help You.* (selected and arranged by Warren Meyer) Unity School of Christianity. 1957, pp. 178-186.

2. Ibid.

3. Letter to Grace Norton, August 9, 1928. Myrtle Fillmore collection, Unity Archives. Unity School of Christianity.

4. "Report of Midweek services," *Unity*, July, 1899, p. 28.

5. Letter to Grace Norton, Op. cit.

6. Letter to Martha Rieck, September 7, 1928. Myrtle Fillmore collection. Unity Archives

7. Letter from Charles to Myrtle. July 16, 1878. Myrtle Fillmore collection. Unity Archives.

8. Letter from Myrtle to Charles. September 1, 1878. Charles S. Fillmore collection, Personal File, Unity Archives.

9. Ibid.

10. Ibid.

11. Ibid.

12. Charles Fillmore, *Autograph Book*, 1879-1881. Unpublished. Charles S. Fillmore collection, Unity Archives.

13. Ibid.

14. Letter from Myrtle to Charles, March 19, 1881. Charles S. Fillmore collection, Personal file, Unity Archives.

15. Ibid.

16. Ibid.

17. Charles S. Fillmore, *Autograph Book*, Op. cit.

18. Notices appeared in "The Henry County Democrat" and "The Clinton Advocate." March, 1881.

19. Gatlin, Op. cit.

20. Ibid.

21. Ibid.

22. Letter from Myrtle to Charles, March 1, 1885. Myrtle Fillmore collection, Unity Archives.

23. Ibid.

24. Ibid.

25. Lowell Fillmore, *Weekly Unity*, May 9, 1954.

26. Gatlin, Op. cit.

27. Ibid.

28. Ibid.

29. Letter from Myrtle to Momsey (Mary G. Fillmore), July 28, 1887. Mary Georgiana Fillmore collection, Unity Archives.

30. Letter from Myrtle to Momsey, August 7, 1887. Mary Georgiana Fillmore collection, Unity Archives.

31. Ibid.

32. Letter from Myrtle to Momsey, August 8, 1887 (addendum to letter of August 7th).

33. Letter from Myrtle to Momsey, August 19, 1887. Mary G. Fillmore collection, Unity Archives.

34. Ibid.

35. Letter from Momsey to Myrtle, Charles and Lowell, August 25, 1887. Myrtle Fillmore collection, Unity Archives.

36. Letter from Myrtle to Momsey, September 11, 1887. Mary G. Fillmore collection, Unity Archives.

37. Ibid.

38. Ibid.

## 8. *Family*

1. Lowell Fillmore, "The Mother of Unity." *Weekly Unity*. May 9, 1954.

2. Ernest Wilson, "Grandma Fillmore: She Brought Things Together." *Unity*, July, 1979.

3. From Myrtle to "my dear, dear, sister," October 29, 1925. Myrtle Fillmore collection, Unity Archives.

4. Ibid.

5. Ibid.

6. Certificate of Death. Missouri State Board of Health. Mrs. Mary G. Fillmore, Date of Death, March 12, 1931. Time 11:11 A.M. Cause of death "anemic endocarditis deficiency." Signed by Dr. Marie Esmond, 1300 Professional Building.

7. Letter to Cousin Lottie, Op. cit.

8. See information on Lowell Fillmore in *The Unity Movement is Evolution and Spiritual Teaching* by Neal Vahle pp. 95-120.

9. See information on Rickert Fillmore in *The Unity Movement is Evolution and Spiritual Teach-*

*ing* by Neal Vahle pp. 181-189.

10. Note from Royal and Frances Fillmore to Myrtle Fillmore, August 6, 1931. Myrtle Fillmore collection, Unity Archives.

11. *Unity News*, September 1, 1923.

12. Letter from a Unity Staff member to Mr. and Mrs. Sleater, September 10, 1923. Royal Fillmore collection, Unity Archives.

13. Letter from Royal Fillmore to Charles and Myrtle Fillmore, September 4, 1923. Charles S. Fillmore collection, Unity Archives.

14. Ibid.

15. Ibid.

16. Telegram from Howard Colby to Mr. and Mrs. Fillmore, September 9, 1923. Charles S. Fillmore collection, Unity Archives.

17. Letter from Unity staff member to Mr. and Mrs. Sleater, Op. cit.

18. Certificate of Death, State of Michigan. Royal Fillmore at Battle Creek Sanitarium, September 9, 1923. Signed by Lloyd B. Verity, M.D. For definitions of Royal's causes of death I consulted *Stedman's Medical Dictionary*. Baltimore: Williams and Wilkins, 1961. Thomas E Witherspoon reported that Royal suffered from diabetes. He wrote that "diabetes and high blood pressure caused him constant pain." I can find no written confirmation that Royal was a diabetic, or that it contributed to his death. Since Witherspoon does not cite the source of this information, it is impossible to check it for accuracy. (See Witherspoon, Thomas. *Myrtle Fillmore, Mother of Unity*. Unity Books, Unity School of Christianity, 1977. p 59.)

19. Telegram from Charles Fillmore to Royal Fillmore, September 7, 1923. Royal Fillmore collection, Unity Archives.

20. Letter from Myrtle to Mabel Lowe, October 26, 1927. Myrtle Fillmore collection, Unity Archives.

21. See information on Charles R. Fillmore in *The Unity Movement is Evolution and Spiritual Teaching* by Neal Vahle pp. 190–195.

22. See information on Rosemary Fillmore Rhea in *The Unity Movement is Evolution and Spiritual Teaching* by Neal Vahle pp. 204–205.

# 9. Passing

1. Letter from Charles Fillmore to Mrs. Mabel Low, October 6, 1931. Charles S. Fillmore collection, Unity Archives.

2. Telephone interview with Frances Lakin, October 12, 1995.

3. Ernest Wilson, "As I Remember Myrtle." *Unity*, March, 1979.

4. Bach, Marcus. *The Unity Way*. Unity Books, Unity School of Christianity, 1982, pp. 124–125.

5. Letter from Lowell Fillmore to H. Emilie Cady, November 17, 1931. Lowell Fillmore collection, Unity Archives.

6. Pearl Duval. Unpublished manuscript, Pearl Duval collection, Unity Archives.

7. Tesla Landon Wallace. Statement given in an unpublished manuscript. Myrtle Fillmore collection, Unity Archives.

8. *Unity*, January, 1932.

9. Letter to Mrs. Pratt, November 10, 1930. Myrtle Fillmore collection, Unity Archives.

10. Letter to Mrs. Armstrong, November 4, 1930. Myrtle Fillmore collection, Unity Archives.

11. Letter to Puella Mason, December 8, 1930. Myrtle Fillmore collection, Unity Archives.

12. Letter to Mrs. Armstrong, January 30, 1931. Myrtle Fillmore collection, Unity Archives.

13. Letter to Mrs. Flint, February 3, 1931. Myrtle Fillmore collection, Unity Archives.

14. Letter to Mrs. Boardman, April 6, 1931. Myrtle Fillmore collection, Unity Archives.

15. Letter to Mrs. Crater, January 31, 1931. Myrtle Fillmore collection, Unity Archives.

16. Letter to Mabel Low, August 14, 1931. Myrtle Fillmore collection, Unity Archives.

17. Letter to Matilda McNemar, August 25, 1931. Myrtle Fillmore collection, Unity Archives.

18. Letter to Lucy Kellerhouse, September 30, 1931. Myrtle Fillmore collection, Unity Archives.

19. Letter to Dr. Benjamin Hauser, April 30, 1931. Myrtle Fillmore collection, Unity Archives.

20. Letter to the Lathops, September 5, 1928. Myrtle Fillmore collection, Unity Archives.

21. Letter to Helen Mack, September 5, 1931. Myrtle Fillmore collection, Unity Archives.

22. Letter to Caroline Risley, September 19, 1928. Myrtle Fillmore collection, Unity Archives.

23. Letter to Mrs. Kent, September 22, 1928. Myrtle Fillmore collection, Unity Archives.

24. Letter to Nellie Wilcox, September 7, 1928. Myrtle Fillmore collection, Unity Archives.

25. Letter to Elizabeth, September 18, 1930. Myrtle Fillmore collection, Unity Archives.

26. Letter to Amelia Murdock Wing, September 18, 1928. Myrtle Fillmore collection, Unity Archives.

27. Letter to Ella F. Helm, September 29, 1928. Myrtle Fillmore collection, Unity Archives.

28. Letter to Sarah Quigley, September 28, 1931. Myrtle Fillmore collection, Unity Archives.

29. "The Passing of Myrtle Fillmore. *Unity*, January, 1932.

30. Letter from Charles Fillmore to Mabel Low, Op. cit.

31. Missouri State Board of Health, Medical Certificate of Death. October 6, 1931. Registered No. 193, Myrtle Fillmore. Signed by Marie Esmond, M.D., 1300 Professional Building. Copy in Myrtle Fillmore collection, Unity Archives.

32. Letter to Marion Irons, August 11, 1931. Myrtle Fillmore collection, Unity Archives.

33, Letters to Aunt Ella, September 1, 1931 and Elizabeth Berlinghoff, September 8, 1931. Myrtle Fillmore collection, Unity Archives.

34. Letter to Mrs. Sarah B. Quigley, September 11, 1931. Myrtle Fillmore collection, Unity Archives.

35. Letter to Helen Mack, September 11, 1931. Myrtle Fillmore collection, Unity Archives.

36. Letter to Clara, December 2, 1929. Myrtle Fillmore collection, Unity Archives.

37. Letter to Lola Jones, September 16, 1931. Myrtle Fillmore collection, Unity Archives.

38. Letter to Laura Bolles, September 16, 1931. Myrtle Fillmore collection, Unity Archives.

39. Letter to Stella Paulus, September 24, 1931. Myrtle Fillmore collection, Unity Archives.

40. Letter to Mary Gerber, September 11, 1931. Myrtle Fillmore collection, Unity Archives.

41. See letters to Lucy Kellerhouse, September 30, 1031, Mary Parrish, September 29, 1931, Donna Smythe, September 22, 1931, Ruth Rae, September 28, 1931. Myrtle Fillmore collection, Unity Archives.

42. Letter to Blanche Haesly, October 5, 1931. Myrtle Fillmore collection, Unity Archives.

43. The six physicians I consulted were: Fred Whinery MD, Dorothy Waddell MD, Sadja Greenwood MD, Allan Margolis MD, Richard Levine MD, and Frances Herb MD. All work in the San Francisco Bay Area. Each is either currently practicing Internal Medicine, or has practiced it in the past.

44. Letter to "My Dear Sister." No date on letter, but information in its contents indicates it was written in early March, 1931. Myrtle Fillmore collection, Unity Archives.

# Appendix One

**M**ost of the existing letters of Myrtle Fillmore were written during the last three and a half years of her life. The twelve in this appendix are examples of the kinds of letters she wrote. They cover the many topics she addressed, and include the wide range of people with whom she corresponded. The letters are not presented chronologically. I have numbered them for the purpose of clearly separating them from each other. The reader will note that Myrtle Fillmore occasionally made errors in spelling and punctuation. For example, she spelled "enclosed" as "inclosed" and "cooperation" as "co-operation." She continually used exclamation marks where they didn't belong, and the use of the comma is not in accord with present practice. Her errors in spelling and punctuation were not corrected in this manuscript.

## Letter Number One

Myrtle Fillmore often wrote very long letters, particularly if the addressee was a new student, as was Grace Norton. In this lengthy letter, covering several pages, Myrtle described her own spiritual journey, the journey that led to the development of the Unity teaching. As in most letters to new students, Myrtle covered important points in the Unity teaching and made suggestions for further reading.[1]

*August 9, 1928*
*Our Dear Grace Norton:*

A part of your letter came to my desk some time ago. But I have allowed more urgent demands upon my time to take my attention, and so have delayed answering that part referring to my recovery. My family, for generations, have been members of the church. They were and are a God-fearing people. I was carefully reared in this Christian atmosphere. But I found that my dear ones did not have an understanding of God, who ruled their lives, that satisfied me. My mother was a very spiritual woman. She always kept the principles of right and love before us by her own example. But she had accepted the church creed. And had such a devotional spirit that she felt that if her God saw fit to punish, or to do any of the many things that were attributed to God, He must have a reason for it and it was all right. I marveled that my wonderful mother who loves so devotedly souls have a God who might punish, or take the lives of His children.

I liked to read books which, in symbol and allegory, I have since learned were efforts of the authors to picture the experiences of the human soul. I delighted in getting out in the garden, or to walk in the woods. I loved to touch a tree; and felt that it was truly intelligent. I received something very satisfying from y close contact with Nature. I know, now, that I was feeling and responding to the omnipresent Spirit of God. And that the abundant Life of God was pouring out to me from everywhere, and that my hungry soul and body were drinking it, and rejoicing to express it.

During my childhood, there was no real understanding of God as the health of His people. And, so, I did not know how to disconnect myself from the hereditary thought of weakness. Some of the members of my family had been weak and some succumbed to the belief in disease. So, because I was a bit different, some of them no doubt began expecting me to show signs of weakness. I may not have had what a child should have to enable it to develop a sturdy body. My intellectual bent may have been partly responsible for my failure to keep in health. After putting myself wholeheartedly into my chosen profession, I (illegible sentence) South to rest and build up. While in the south, I yielded to persuasions to teach a small school which was arranged for me.

There, I met the man who was destined to catch this spiritual vision with me, and we were married. But owing to lack of understanding of the health law, neighbor of us were as strong as we should have been to manage a home and bring forth children. I suffered, and the children suffered, and the burdens affected Mr. Fillmore's health, which had never been really good. All this while, I kept feeling that there was a way of life which could be discovered, and that would insure happiness and health and plenty. We had the opportunity to investigate what was then known as Christian Science. My receptive mind and heart kept me catching at the ideas which appealed to my reason and my intuition. After a while I was convinced that god would not create a world in which sickness and sorrow and lack had a part.

I knew that god, whom I could call Father, would not create imperfect children. And as I thought of it, I began to realize that I was truly God's child, and that because of this, I must of necessity inherit from Him. Then, because the very Spirit of God is in man, I began to wake up, and Spirit began to illumine my consciousness, and I saw that the life that is in us is the Life of god. Then, I reasoned, the plan of God must be an inherent part of the mind of man. And since I had learned to live in books, and with the trees, I began to live with God, and to talk with Him just as I had talked with these familiar things about me. And god revealed to me that my body was intelligent, and that I could direct it, and praise it, and it would respond. I just assumed that God was hearing me, and answering my prayers. That He was giving me His Life and substance and intelligence, and that

I was to use them, even more freely than I had used the blessings my earthly father had given me.

I didn't get entirely well and strong all at once. And there were a few times, after my first discoveries and healings, when I felt the need to hold on tight. There was one time, when the household duties fell upon me, with the small children to care for. I felt the old familiar heaviness, and pain, and smothering in the chest and aching all through the body. I do not know why I felt as I did—that I should throw myself into housecleaning with all the strength I could muster. But that is just what I did. I went upstairs, swept room after room, rearranged and set in order all that part of the house, with windows wide open, and perspiration flowing. I noted that I began to feel relaxed, and to breathe easier. I kept holding that God my Father was my health and strength. I did not have pneumonia. But I am not advising that others should take this as a suggestion in the treatment of such appearances!

Along with the tubercular trouble in lungs, I had disorders through the abdominal walls. At times, hemorrhoids made life miserable. Because this abdominal trouble had a definite cause in the realm of my own mental attitudes, it was necessary for me to grow in understanding and to make definite changes, to bring about healing. The trouble didn't respond to ordinary faith and prayer. I finally asked the Lord just why it was that I did not get well. I explained in my communion that I had gone all through my consciousness, to see what it was that held me, and that I had tried to find the fault.

The Spirit said to me, "You have looked among your faults; now look among your virtues." I thought it strange, but soon it came to me that I had to keep my feelings to myself; taking great pride in the fact that I never let any one know just how I felt, or that anything displeased me or hurt me. I found that I didn't feel as sweet and poised on the inside as I seemed outwardly. I began to watch, and to redeem this state of mind. I determined to handle all that came to me, before I "swallowed it" and allowed it to irritate and cut and weaken my nerves and organs. As I gained real poise, and the ability to keep my thoughts and feelings truly free, I was healed and restored to strength and normal functioning. But as time went on I learned that if I dared slip back into the old habit of letting some personal grievance or annoyance settle down in my soul, the inner intelligence would give me a warning. The enclosed pamphlet will give you a little more of the method of treatment employed here at the School. This article is based on my own early experience.

I will say that in those early days, I hardly knew just what was taking place, as the were accomplished. I only know that my experience was much like that of the blind man whom Jesus healed: "One thing I know, that, whereas I was blind, now I see." I simply had great faith that God, the loving Father, who had so marvelously revealed himself to me as my help in every need, and my faith inspired others to have faith— and "Faith is the substance of things hoped for; the evidence of things not seen". And I was always glad to pray for those who sought my help. I do not think that the success of the prayers was do to their word formations. Sometimes I merely assured those who came that I believed God could and would help them. At the time, healing seemed the most important thing in life to me; and I loved seeing folks get well, and happy. I do yet; but I have learned that the spiritual awakening, and the daily development of Christ powers are more important. The soul must be awakened, and brought to a realization of the Truth, and encouraged in the righteous use of all the God-given faculties and powers. The individual must be helped to unify his spirit, soul, and body, in harmonious spiritual living here and now. health is a result—the outpicturing of the expression of Christ ideas in thought, word and act.

There is nothing in the part of your letter that I have, to indicate that you are acquainted with our Silent Unity work—so, I am inclosing a tract, explaining the work of the Silent Unity. it was grown in numbers since the tract was printed in 1926, but the work is carried on much the same. I note that the Editorial Department has checked your request for more information regarding the growing of a new and third set of teeth. So, I shall not go into that in detail. Teeth suffer because of some form of waste. It may be prompted by belief in life as material. And due to lack of understanding of the law of life and health and conservation. It may be misuse of the life forces through disobedience along conjugal lines; failing to understand and live as divinely planned with regard to pro-creation. It may be failure to understand how to properly feed the body with foods required by the various tissue masses.

So, the work of renewing the system, to the end that all the tissues and organs and members may be renewed and perfected, must proceed along several lines. Study to understand the Truth of being first. Positive and regular and consistent identification with God through the Christ within. Obedience to the three-fold law of life and health and harmony. Doing always that which is truly best for the individual, and indirectly for society. Taking good care of the physical—living scientifically, knowing just what is required, and just when to appropriate food and drink to best advantage. Having a good practical working plan for your life's expression, and improving this from time to time as it is found advisable. Growth in all ways is one of the requirements of health and youth, and the perfect functioning of the body.

We do not go into the details of physical care and diet, in our letters or literature. But we do give individual attention to these things, and sometimes suggest to those writing us that they do the same. We find it helpful sometimes, to get to those who are specializing in this phase of healing and maintaining health, for points on which we may not be clear. On a separate slip we are sending you the address of one who can give you simple and practical help with diet. He has studied the chemical content of the body, and the foods supplying the elements required.

A knowledge of the combinations to stir up the life-giving and bone renewing processes in the organism should prove helpful in growing new teeth. We appreciate the fact that you are getting at these things, and trust that the suggestions we have given will help. But your own study, and declaration of God--given wisdom and life and light and power will help you more. What others do is of little real lasting benefit, except it may prompt you to develop your own consciousness. But don't let this keep you from searching, or writing, or gaining knowledge in any way you can—your reaching for Truth opens the doors and the ideas of divine Mind flood in.

*Yours in love and Truth,*

## Letter Number Two

Many of Myrtle's letters were to personal friends. This letter is to a former secretary, a young woman she corresponded with regularly. In addition to fulfilling a request for advice Myrtle provided news about the goings-on at Unity headquarters, gave information about Unity workers, anecdotes about her grandchildren, and personal information about herself.

*September 28, 1931*
*Mrs. Sarah B. Quigley,*
*My Dear Quiggie:*

I was glad of a real letter from a past secretary. I get one from Miss Millie Chandler every once in a while. She's spicy, isn't she? I had some other reports of Louise Newman's yearly conference—good, very good, according to most of these reports. I think, my dear, you have not gotten away from some of your old time grudges, which you understand, do not or should not find place at a gathering of regenerate souls.

Dearie, that is something I am trying to cleanse my heart of—remembering some things that have tang of bitterness. I am progressing but I am not an angel yet. There is really so much weeding to do before "I behold the Christ in you" that I am giving my own "garden" much attention now. We've a lovely set of people attending our training school this year, from several foreign countries as well as most of our home states. Few have taken in the full course. The school teachers, of which we had a number, left the first of September. Some were from universities. Most of the students had a great desire to fit themselves for the Field; some were very interesting and remarkable people. A linguist from Washington, D.C., one of her friends said, was writing her morning lessons in six languages. Just think! she wrote her lessons in six different languages! She has been here nearly the whole time.

The earnestness and appreciation of those that have been here is quite wonderful. The little petty things people talk so much of usually, have been noted for their absence. You know, dear Quiggie, when we keep looking fort the "Image and likeness" o f Him we serve, we find little else. You will rejoice in seeing how our E.V. Ingraham has grown. It is encouraging to see the strides he makes. Mr. Jeffery too is wonderful. All our teachers have their special radiance.

There has been more excitement and fun than usual lately among the children. The reason for this is that "Sandy," little Charles Rickert's dog has had "an increase in family." There were five and each a different "pattern". Little Rosemary is helping Sandy be a mother to all this brood, and on nice days she takes them all out in the sunshine for an airing, and in the evening puts them all to bed. It would tickle you pink to watch her. We have had as much fun watching the children as they have had playing with the dog's children, so "everybody's happy."

It has been so long since you've seen the children that you'd hardly know them. Fran will be ten years old the first day of October. If you were here now Rosemary would treat you to something funny—when company comes, she makes the puppies have their dinner. When Mr. and Mrs. Hill were with me this morning we stopped at Rick's, and Rosemary was playing with her pets, and she wanted us to see how they "sat at the table."

*Bless you, Quiggie dear,*
*Lovingly yoÏΪ\urs*

## Letter Number Three

The Landon family were personal friends of the Fillmores, dating back to the early days of the movement. In this letter Myrtle gets right to the point, in responding to a young man she had known for several years. He evidently was suffering from the economic consequences of the Great Depression.

*September 17, 1931*
*Mr. Herald S. Landon,*
*My blessed Boy:*

Your call for "a lesson from me" is just received—and you shall have it, with all my heart. I think the disappointments and unhappy experiences are just opportunities for you to put what you know of Truth to the test, so that you will grow stronger and more full of faith, and thus be ready for greater blessings that are on the way. Do not take those experiences too seriously—they come to all of us who have not attained the Jesus Christ mastery over circumstances. Take what comfort you can in the knowledge that "they too shall pass away," to give place to a bright outlook and a new period of success.

By meeting all the little troubles with a spirit of courage, good temper, optimism, you will bring to the surface those God-given qualities and capabilities which will enable you to accomplish really big and worth-while things. The purpose of life is to develop and bring into righteous expression all of the living qualities implanted in the soul, and not count success in dollars and cents. The dollars will come after the individual has unfolded the capabilities that demonstrate material prosperity, that are the very foundation of outer success.

So when you have times when everything seems to go wrong, learn to "count it all joy." Such times cannot last very long and they will pass away sooner when you meet every situation from the foundation of Truth, to create your own breaks. You are spiritually alive, alert, awake and efficient, ready to make your own opportunities. You may be sure that we are not at all worrying about your pledge to the Temple fund; neither should you let it disturb you. "In nothing be anxious."

*Love to you and all the dear ones,*

## Letter Number Four

In this letter Myrtle gives marital advice to a Unity center leader from Dallas, Texas, a woman who was also a personal friend. In the opening paragraph Myrtle suggests that her friend follow her own inner guidance in dealing with the problem. As the letter progresses, however, Myrtle forcefully argues for her leaving the marriage.

*May 22, 1931*
*Mrs. Minerva L. Hursey,*
*My very dear Friend:*

You are asking me questions, that while I have my own answers from my own point of understanding, still I feel that this that you are dealing with, must come from your own highest conviction of what the Father's will directs. So far as I can decide, if I were concerned in a problem like yours, I would have tried even as you, to have found a point of harmony and agreement; but my own dear, patient sister, you have suffered far beyond the limit of patient endurance, and have let yourself become an ally to his selfish desires.

You are a brave, upright sou. "Thy Maker is thy husband; Jehovah of hosts is his name." Can you not, then, see that you are free and must give him freedom to go his way? You have nothing in common. Why should you make a doormat for a man who chooses you no longer, either as wife or companion? Why should you labor to support a woman, for your husband, who really fills all the offices of his wants? Let him go his way. Give him his freedom, his divorce. Let God take care of his case; it's no longer your business to meddle with it. Be yourself! Give him back his name, even, and go about the Father's business. You will find yourself freed from the burden of trying to save him. He must save himself.

People love you because you love and bless everybody. Do what is best. Ask the Father; He will show you. Your way is to make "straight the way of the Lord," and your affairs will straighten out as God would have them. A woman who had known you and respected you, told me once that you were spoiling much of good, influential work by having in your home a woman for your husband. I do not listen to gossip. People are always apparently ready to misinterpret what they do not understand. It is right for you to have help in your home, you must have when you have other work to do. But why should it make gossip? You have told me many things I could not or would not brook, or think I would not, in my home.

I can see, dear friend, while you were striving to overcome the painful and disagreeable things connected with your home service, other people saw only what you were letting pass, as things you encouraged. I do not like, dear friend, to litter my message up with this kind of error. I believe in you. I believe you have let yourself be crucified, that good may come. But have you agreed in your heart that it really benefited yourself or anybody else? No. I think not, according to this letter. Well then, take your stand AND STAND! Save yourself first. Infinite wisdom guides you, Divine love strengthens, uplifts and sustains you, and all your affairs are brought into perfect order. The Lord bless you and keep you.

*Lovingly, in His Name,*

## Letter Number Five

Myrtle's correspondent is Fannie Wingate, a friend with whom she corresponded regularly. Myrtle acknowledges Fannie for work accomplished and provides encouragement for the challenges still ahead. In this letter she focuses on the nature of love, providing insights and suggestions.

*September 19, 1930*
*Our dear Fannie Wingate:*

Why, of course we knew it would come—"that happiness report!" When I wrote my last letter to you, I had a wonderful silence in which I saw such glorious things for you. And somehow the Spirit gave me the inner conviction that they were coming to pass; really, they became substance right then and there. I just knew that your good was manifest—no two ways about it. I love to think about how much you have overcome and how splendidly you are growing spiritually. Your faith in your Divine "image and likeness," implanted in you from the beginning, is bringing forth its works.

The Master said that he came into the world not to be ministered unto, but to minister. He did not seek to be loved by others, merely to satisfy the human desire for affection; His great purpose was to love. He radiated love like the sun radiates light. It may seem strange but the Law works that way—by being anxious for love, and more or less selfishly desiring that others love us, we tend to keep love in its fullness away. But when we put aside all striving for affection, and give our attention to expressing love toward everybody and everything, then love comes to us without seeking. "Love seeketh not her own." Love attracts its own and does not have to strive for anything.

Your little poem, "Happy Day," in the September UNITY DAILY WORD is very sweet and beautiful. Perhaps you are going to read it in Brandenton. Through the Spirit of the Lord within you are more than equal to every occasion, so your evening of readings is going to be a glorious success. We are getting ready for another intensive training school that will begin October 20. No doubt our Publishing Department has already sent you a program, but in case they haven't, I shall inclose one.

Your love gift is rich in the bountiful consciousness in which you sent it, and that came with it. Your rich consciousness demonstrates plenty in your own world, and blesses all whom you contact. We thank you and bless you. Next week is going to be Silent Unity's "Faith Week;" we are going to give special emphasis to the bringing forth of faith. Faith will be the one BIG IDEA we shall hold in mind. We lovingly invite you to join with us, and we know that you are bound to get results.

*Always lovingly,*

## Letter Number Six

This long letter is typical of the kind Myrtle wrote to a new Unity student. While Myrtle assumes the role of spiritual teacher in all of her letters, she plays that role most fully in correspondence with new students. She outlines several Truth Principles, including: the nature of the divine, the importance of "right thought," the need to discipline the mind, the use of affirmations, the elements of spiritual healing, the power of prayer, and the importance of a cleansing and eliminative diet."

*October 18, 1928*
*Our Dear Mrs. Taylor:*

I am glad the account of some of my personal experiences has found its way into your hands, and your mind, and heart! Indeed I will proclaim for you the Light and the Life and the Substance, omnipresent, ever active, all-sufficient, ready to meet your needs and to keep you in the divine order and harmony which the Creator intends. Now, read this statement over again, and then proclaim it with me—that is:

"God in me is the Light, the Life, the Substance, the Power, omnipresent, ever active, all-sufficient, and ready to meet my every need, and to restore, and keep me in the divine order and harmony which He has crated. I now relax, and become receptive to new ideas, and the spiritual direction of all that pertains to my life, that I may rest in Him, and work in Him, and fulfill His plan in all my daily living. I gladly give up my old habits of will and living, that I may be renewed in soul and in body, and that I may use all my faculties to the glory of God."

Now let us know that God has heard and is answering our prayer, and working through you and for you in all ways to cleanse, to renew, to rebuild, to perfect, to establish perfect order and harmony throughout your system. Then, let us do our part, in looking into our daily thought habits, and our daily living habits, to see that we are doing that which is truly in accord with His will and plan. Are you relaxing several times a day—just to let your thoughts become equalized, and poised in Truth? Are you letting go of all strain and all worry and all effort at study—so that your circulation will become equalized? Are you faithfully giving up old negative thoughts as fast as new light reveals them to you? Are you continuing to go to the doctors or surgeons, or to take their treatment? This doesn't make any difference to us, of course—but it does make a great difference to you. For so long as your faith is centered in someone or something outside of yourself you will depend on that, and fail to turn to God and receive the new ideas and act upon them, to get real results.

The trouble in throat, ears, face, and eyes and the rheumatism are all from the same general causes—mental and physical. Your mind has been full of conflicting opinions and desires; and you have long felt that persons and things outside of yourself affect you or hinder your good. You have tried through personal will to bring order into your life, and to accomplish that which you have desired to do. At the same time, you have lost control in your body, and have turned it over to the experiments of others. Now, you are consecrating your mind and your heart and your body to God. And we are helping you to learn His law of life and health and joy. Old thoughts, old conditions are as waters that have passed away. The Lord in you is now making all things new.

146

You sent the band, asking us to bless it. But, Dear, you have placed such a limitation on that band, that we are not going to bless it in the way that you had expected! We are going to bless it, for you to use as "quilt pieces" or to throw into the waste basket! The very idea of your asking us to bless that band—so you can "use it always!" Don't you see how ridiculous that is, when you are coming to us, to god, for healing? I think you do; and that you will enjoy a good laugh with us, right now! The blessing, and the healing aren't in any magic words which we say over a piece of cloth, or a paper, or in any magic spell which we create through prayer. The healing and the quickening and freeing power are in your own soul. God Mind finds you receptive to its power and love and light and life, and it flows in, to transform you! We are witnessing this transformation which is now taking place in you. Because there is only the one Mind; and all of us have consciousness in that one Mind, we do daily join you, faithfully, in proclaiming the Truth, and in giving thanks, and in rejoicing for the blessings we have asked. We even take lists bearing the names of all those who write us for help, and hold them in our hands, and read them, and bless them, daily—for we know that all those folks are present with us, and joining with us, and receiving the blessings we and they are declaring and expecting. But it is the individual's own receptivity, his own recognition, his own expectation, his own use of what God is, that brings the good results.

Now, in connection with the treatment we are giving you, we advise that you give attention to your daily diet. You will find it very helpful, to supply the food elements required by your system in its daily work, and in the elimination of any possible accumulations, which may be causing congestion. Just now, a regular cleansing, or eliminative diet—a regular feasting of fresh citrus fruits, and grapes and apples and pears, and of fresh green vegetables—over a period of seven days, will be splendid for you. Lemon juice in water, and an occasional glass of orange juice—so that you take 10 or 12 of these fruits a day—will quickly relieve the heavy dull feelings, and the pain in head and eyes. It will furnish your blood with what it requires, to properly cleanse and vitalize the cell structures.

After the feasting on fruits and green vegetables, a proper daily building diet will keep you in health and comfort. And avoiding too much of certain foods will keep your system clear of the elements which are accumulating and causing the sinus trouble and the trouble in the joints. If you are in the habit of drinking coffee or tea, drop these, and take instead a nice large glass of orange juice, or a lemonade, or just clear cold water. There is nothing wrong with your head—it is just trying to make the best of conditions you have caused, and which you can change. Bless that head of yours—that's where the blessing is going to do good—and it will respond and do the splendid work the Father has created it to do! Teach yourself

147

to think only the good and the true about your life, and life in general. There may at times be appearances that seem not good and not true to Truth—but you do not need to think on those things. You can train your mind and heart to think and to feel in perfect accord with Christ ideas, and to mentally transform whatever seems in any way lacking in the expression of the God-given pattern.

For one thing, you have allowed outside suggestions, and sensations in your body, to make you believe that there is something in the weather that causes you suffering. This is not desirable, nor true. Cold air is invigorating. There is nothing but God, and good in the air. And nothing but God, the good in you. And that which is without, and that which is within are harmonious—one. True, the cool air comes to your body, as a tonic and stimulant, and it stirs up the circulation. And if you are inclined to shrink from changes, it causes tension, which results in pain. But you are directing new currents of abundant life into every part of your body now; and giving up the old beliefs, and so, you must welcome the cool fresh air, and bless it, and appreciate what it is doing. Tell your skin, your blood stream, your muscles, your bones, your joints, your glands, your nerves, your lungs, your throat, eyes, ears, face, forehead, every part of your body, that God is abiding within and furnishing everything required to keep them in perfect health; and that God has given the cool fresh air as a great blessing, which each and every part is to benefit by and enjoy.

Get out in the air daily, relax, and let every part of the body pulse with the abundant life, and take advantage of the exercise, and the air. You will find that each day gives you more freedom and courage, and more vigor, and more joy. When you come in from a nice walk, take a cup of warm vegetable broth, and curl up for a little nap. You will wake up, feeling like the new creature that you are! Remember now, you are to forget the past, and its mistakes and worries. Ask your dear body to forgive you for the doctoring and neglect. And promise it that you will better understand its needs, and supply them, and that you will daily help by your right mental attitude, and your wise living habits, to make it the radiant temple the Creator intends. You are not to equalize your life forces, and will not need a band to restrain the pulsing of the life which was only trying to regulate and restore harmony.

Use the band you had undoubtedly planned to "use always", for tying up your rose-bushes, or morning glories, or cauliflower leaves, or for mending, or quilt blocks,—anything to put it to god use! We have blessed it to do a good work—in any one of the above places! But your head—why the glory of God's own life and light and love is there. And the divine pattern of the Father's own perfect child gives your head the freedom, and poise, and comfort, and purity, and keenness of functioning, and beauty of substance. Our blessing for you is a living, vital consciousness of health and joy and ability. Remember, we are with you, and you are with us, receiving our blessing, all the time your thinking is in accord with Truth. You are in touch with, and abiding in infinite Good all the time.

The inclosed Instructions will give you further help in co-operating with us. And you will note that we expect a report from you, within a month from this time. You see, we expect splendid reports always, and we like to give our friends and students the opportunity to acknowledge their healings.

*Yours in Love and Truth,*

## Letter Number Seven

In this letter Myrtle outlines her ideas on regeneration and sexual relationships to a woman who apparently is writing to Unity for the first time. She tells her correspondent, in typically direct Myrtle Fillmore fashion, that she is avoiding "flowery language" and giving it "straight from the shoulder."

*March 21, 1930*
*Our dear Mrs. Hazelhurst:*

At your request your letter was handed to me by Silent Unity. We are praying for you and yours faithfully. We are inclosing for you some of our booklets that will answer many of the questions you asked regarding sex matters. Study them thoroughly, and ask the Spirit of Truth to illumine your consciousness, so that you will grasp the inner meaning of the words you read. Spiritual things are spiritually discerned.

Unity teaches the regeneration taught and demonstrated by Jesus Christ, and all who aspire to eternal health and prosperity, and even eternal life here and now, are accepting the way of regeneration. Our mission at Unity is to give the Jesus Christ teaching in its purity. People are free to choose their own destiny—those who desire to continue in generation may do so, for unity does not try to force Christ principles upon anyone. Those who are seeking the higher way that leads to eternal life are receiving the blessings that come through fulfilling spiritual law. My experience has been that Mr. Fillmore and I have been a great help to each other. We prayed and meditated together in the silence holding the same prayers, the law governing regeneration gradually unfolded to us.

Sex passion is a taint; it is lust that sets the cells of the body on fire, which causes death. Lust is the result of men and women thinking that true spiritual intercourse is a thing apart from the Lord. Paul said, "Do all things unto the Lord." This means that we should submit every thought and every act to the Divine Law. When men and women do this a holy intercourse will ensue, and the immaculate conception takes place, instead of the usual conception through lust in sin. When immaculate conception takes place children will be born healthy just as Jesus was; then the regeneration of the body naturally will follow. Joseph did not know Mary carnally—that is, in lust, but he was necessary to the bringing forth of Jesus under the inspiration of the Holy Spirit. This may seem mystical to people in sense consciousness, but it is the true interpretation of the Scriptures over which there is so much contention in Biblical circles. We do not condemn generation; it is all right for those who are not highly evolved sufficiently to accept and understand regeneration. When the sex force is purified, uplifted and consecrated to the Lord, it maintains the body in health, youth, strength; it quickens the mental and spiritual faculties and makes the mind alert, keen, and capable of discerning the deep things of Spirit. It makes the soul radiant and the body alive.

The world needs souls who demonstrate Christ principles. Thousands of children are born to those who are not yet ready for the regeneration, to those who see nothing higher than gratifying the lusts of the flesh. One need not worry about the world not being populated. If your children desire to know about the regeneration, explain it to them, but do not try to force it upon them. When the soul is ready the way to higher things will open for it. We sent you the book, "TALKS TO MEN." The inclosed literature covers points that "TALKS TO MEN" does not fully explain.

Pray for the guidance of the Holy Spirit, and the Truth will unfold to you as fast as you are able to receive it. We set you free to do as you are led from within to do. We thank you heartily for the love gift. We place the blessing of abundant increase on your finances and on all your good, that you may be enriched bountifully in all your ways. We have tried to avoid flowery language and to give you the Truth "straight from the shoulder." We trust that the letter and the literature will clear up all the questions you had in mind relative to the righteous use of the creative forces. May God's rich blessings be poured out upon you and yours in bountiful measure.

*Faithfully yours,*

## Letter Number Eight

Many people with problems in finding rewarding and remunerative work wrote to Myrtle for advice and help. In this lengthy letter, written to an occasional correspondent, Myrtle addressed the writer's faulty thinking regarding the search for gainful employment, and emphasized the importance of being in contact with the God within. She warned against negativity, stressed the need to develop the Christ consciousness, and made a strong case for being in service to others.

*May 19, 1929*
*Our Dear Benj. G. Lee:*

It's about time we had a word from you folks. And why hesitate to write us for co-operation in prayer, and for the suggestions which we offer that may turn your faith in just the right direction and clear your vision to the Good that is even now awaiting development and use? We are glad to join you in the earnest endeavor to develop your consciousness, and your talents, and your loving services to the place where you need only acknowledge God Mind as containing the Ideas you need, and then lay hold of them and make practical application and bring forth the blessings.

Yes, I think you do understand what you mean, when you say it almost seems a lack of faith in the Christ within, to seek help through anyone else. but you will remember that Jesus called his twelve disciples, and asked them to join him in his ministry; and in Gethsemane, he asked the disciples to stay awake and pray with him. Have you gone beyond where Jesus was at those times? Now, let's take up this matter of finding an outlet for your abilities, and of meeting the obligations of the home, and providing the things needed day by day. I'm going to pounce on one paragraph of your letter. "There must be one position somewhere of the type or character to which I have been accustomed. The door closes on every one I go after." Now, just look at what you've said, and try to understand the mental attitude that is back of it! See anything which isn't just as the man functioning in the Christ consciousness would express? Study it a bit, and I am sure you will see something; and that you will open to a great Light!

First of all, you narrow the channel of service and expression and supply to "one position". Second, you want that one to be "of the type or character to which you have been accustomed." Want to stay in the same rut always? Aren't you willing to let the spirit of God in you draw you out in different phases of expression and development? You have accustomed yourself to certain ways, and acts, and returns; and you don't want to be shaken out of those habits! But it would appear that Spirit has taken a hand, and is insisting that you do look a little deeper into this Storehouse of Mind and Substance and Love, and launch out in a different course of action and service and growth!

There's pride here, you see; and personal ambition, and set ways—all of which work against real spiritual progress, and greater service, and prosperity. Your study of Truth and your faithful affirmation of the truths you feel to be taking root in your consciousness are making it necessary for you to make adjustments in your actual application, and your living habits. It seems a calamity, only because you haven't looked at circumstances in the light of Spirit. Jesus says, "He that is greatest among you shall be your servant. And whosoever shall exalt himself shall be humbled; and whosoever shall humble himself shall be exalted." Think about the words of Jesus. Spirit will show you what they mean to you.

You know very well that there is much that you can do to help your fellowmen. Get at it, without regard to money returns. What you do for God, God can and will compensate you for. If your ability and training and experience have made you a valuable man, give this valuable service to God, and to His children, in whatever places and ways it is needed. You will find that as you launch out in faith and love, you will open the channels of supply and clear the way for the manifestation of abundance. Instead of sitting, waiting for a certain kind of position, with guarantee of certain salary; instead of writing and phoning, and calling on men, in the hope of interesting them and securing employment, get right out, determined t find just the right place through which to give your services. When you find it, take it, and give the best there is in you—without a thought of the returns! You won't be wasting your time, if you are actually filling a place of real service; and your own faith and love and good work will clear the way for the divine adjustment and compensation.

But don't think that you must keep on with the same line you have been following! If it were in demand, and if your present needs for expression were in that line, you would be working. So, give this old expression into the keeping of the Father, and make known your willingness to take up whatever is for your good and for the good of those with whom you will work. Cease to measure your worth by what you have accomplished n the past. Cease to judge your prosperity by the world's standards. Cease to feel that your home and its security are depending on your personal efforts; these are God's gifts of Love to you and your family! See to it, then that your own heart and mind are filled with divine love and unselfishness and trust, so that you can fill that home with the Spirit of love and good-will and helpfulness, which will be an inspiration to those whom the Father will bring to your home. The home is not yours, to hold for your family, only, you know—but it is a radiating center, through which the Father can bless His children—many of them.

Speaking of the efforts to raise money, or to save the home, or to dispose of it. Why not ask God to use it, as He wills? Why not make yourselves real servants of Christ, and seek to do through your home environment, that which will truly bless and help His little ones? Why not use that home, hourly, to pour out love and blessings. A home that is consecrated to God's use will never prove a burden. And those who give themselves to a loving service and expression which the spirit of Christ love and wisdom will not be weary or discouraged, nor make a failure. I am not thinking of a particular ministry—but just that the home be recognized as an opportunity, and that one or both of you enter upon some real loving service to your community, or city, or even state.

There is great need of many things that may be done by those who are gifted as you and Ellen are. There is great need of the touch which you, and Ellen, and the children can give to those who have not known how to take advantage of their opportunities as you have. That which the Spirit of God is in, he prospers. We are praying with you and for you; with Ellen and for Ellen;' that you may clear away the shadows of past experience and personal limitations and prejudices; and all the Light of god's Presence and Plan flood your consciousness, and lead you forth in ways of pleasantness and paths of peace.

*(Last paragraph and salutation missing)*

## Letter Number Nine

In this letter to a woman with whom she corresponded only on occasion, Myrtle outlines the elements of spiritual healing, including the co-partnership with God. She also emphasizes the value of healing thoughts and ideas, the importance of denials, and argues for the use of powerful words and the necessity of strong faith.

*December 10, 1930*
*Our dear Louise Wardell:*

Of course we remember you, and are very glad to hear from you. "According to your faith be it done unto you:" and your faith has made you whole. We are uniting in prayers with yours and with our spiritual eye of faith, we see you already made whole. Just because the doctor says you "have something" is no real reason that there is anything seriously wrong, you know. God, the Great Physician, proclaims your wholeness, and you can depend upon Him. His word is life and health.

Deny out of both your consciousness and your subconscious, all thought of fear in all its phases, along every line. It came to me a new way of putting this healing of the body, is to remember our co-partnership with the Father was to bring forth into expression the ideas of His perfect creations. "In the beginning, God created," it is written. And God is still creating this perfect idea of man, and we are His sons, restoring His perfect idea to the world. Your own thinking is the formative power of God in action. So when you keep the pattern of a whole and perfect body habitually before your mind's eye and use your word to bring forth that which you discern spiritually, there will be no room for negativeness to enter.

But you know the Law, and all you need is the assurance that the all-powerful Word is being spoken with you and for you, lovingly and faithfully. You are getting rid of some old thoughts, and old cells, and are incorporating some new ideas and radiant health and pure cells into your being. During this "housecleaning" time be busy getting your ideas in order and in harmonious relation, and rejoice that you are every whit whole.

*Lovingly yours,*

## Letter Number Ten

Myrtle often wrote about the nature of God, the power of thought, and the importance of prayer. She touches upon these subjects in this letter to a new student.

*April 16, 1930*
*Our dear Pansy Wilson:*

You are a child of God, and God's love for you is without end. "God is love." He is your help in every need. No longer think of yourself as being sinful; always think of yourself as being a pure, truthful, honest child of God. God did not create you wicked and sinful; He created you in His "image and likeness"—perfection. Begin right now to be very faithful every day to prayer; ask God to give you wisdom and to give you the strength of character to be good, pure, truthful in all your ways. God is more willing to bless you than you are to receive of His blessings.

Your part is to learn how to receive. God has put into your soul wisdom, purity, truthfulness, love, kindness, gentleness—they are a part of you. Now what you are to do, dear child of God, is to have faith in your innate goodness. Think often every day about all the wonderful, Christian qualities that you want to express; the more you think about these qualities and realize that they are already yours, the greater will be your expression of them.

If a thought comes into your mind to tell a lie, put it out of your mind, and take a firm stand for the good and the truth. Jesus said that He came to call the sinners to repentance, to save the sinners and not the righteous. His words are, "There shall be joy in heaven over one sinner that repenteth, more than over ninety and nine righteous persons, who need no repentance." God has given you power to direct your thoughts in ways of purity, righteousness, Truth. Now that you have repented, decided to change your ways for the good, you are becoming "a new creature in Christ Jesus." Silent Unity is praying with you and for you, and I am co-operating with them in prayer. We include your dear mother and the other kind people you mentioned, also. Forgive yourself, and rejoice in God's love and saving power. God blesses you and we bless you.

*Yours in Love and Truth*

## Letter Number Eleven

In this letter to a regular woman correspondent, who used medicine to cure a cold, Myrtle urges the practice of Truth principles and a proper diet.

*August 28, 1931*
*Miss Jean Wilson,*
*Our Dear Jean:*

I could scarcely believe my eyes when I read in your letter an acknowledgment of defeat. Why do you do such a thing? Do you not realize that through the power of God in the midst of you, you can do all things? Then why entertain the belief in defeat? I won't for a moment think that my Jean will let herself believe that a cold is greater than she is—a child of Almightiness, a child of Omnipotent Health.

Rather than "resort to drugs" why don't you give attention to proper diet? Consult a good, reliable dietitian and follow his suggestions, in the selection of your food. Probably you are eating too much acid-forming food, and need citrus fruit, such as limes, lemons, oranges to put the proper elements into your blood stream. Evidently you need to cleanse your system of an accumulation of dead, useless cell material, that prevents your voice from being clear, because the way for its expression is obstructed by the waste matter.

Of course, to be permanently healed, you must spiritualize your mentality, and fill your body temple with the life of Spirit. By eating only those foods that your system requires, you will keep your organism free from the accumulation of obstructing material that interferes with the free flow of the life stream. Keep your mind free from anxiety, and relax all tenseness in your body. Practice the Truth principles in all the details of daily thinking and living, because these details go to make up the whole of living. You are working out your salvation from limitations of every kind, through the help of "Christ in you, the hope of glory. We are blessing you daily with our love and prayers, and have marked for you some very practical helps in the inclosed booklet.

*Yours in loving co-operation,*

## Letter Number Twelve

Myrtle enjoyed reaching out to those who had only recently discovered Unity and expressed an interest in learning more about it. In this long letter to a woman who heard about the movement from a friend, Myrtle outlined several Unity principles, explaining some of the basic elements of Unity teaching. She discussed the nature of God, the need for spiritual awakening, the operation of divine law, the practice of spiritual healing, the use of prayer, the power of thought, the problems associated with the subconscious mind, the value of spiritual ideas, and the importance of proper eating habits. Myrtle encouraged the woman to use the affirmations she enclosed with the letter, and suggested that the woman come to Unity headquarters for further study.

*October 24, 1928*
*Dear Mrs. McAllister:*

We are so glad to learn more of you, and to know that you are enjoying and gaining some spiritual food from your reading of our Unity literature. One of your friends, Mrs. Martha Walker, has written me of you, and has spoken of your need of spiritual understanding of the healing power and presence of God. She also mentioned that Mr. McAllister had been in Kansas City, attending the General Conference, and that you had asked him to attend a Unity meeting. We trust that he was able to come out for one of the Sunday morning services, so that he heard Mr. Fillmore's talk, and the other parts of the program, so that he was able to give you a good idea of our ministry. The small weekday classes are for training in certain phases of Truth, and would hardly give the visitor a good clear idea of the Unity teaching. I am interested to learn that you are a member of the Methodist Episcopal church. I was brought up in a Methodist home and in the Methodist church, though I never became a member myself. But I know that my life must express many of the splendid ideals embodied in the Methodist faith. And I always have a very warm spot in my heart for all Methodist people!

Now, to refer to the condition from which Mrs. Walker says you desire freedom. There is no such thing as a "disease" or an incurable condition in the system. These activities, or weaknesses, or abnormalities, to which the medical profession gives names, are but the efforts of the God-given inner intelligence to deal with conditions which the individual has produced by his failure to understand the Truth and to recognize himself as the perfect child of god, and to live by the divine law of life. Anything which does not measure up to the Christ pattern of perfection can be changed. Anything which the Ideas of God Mind, expressing in the mind of man, have not produced can be dissolved into the original nothingness, by the understanding application of the power of spiritual thought and the resultant spiritual action. First of all, let's just admit that the doctors are judging by appearances, founding their opinions upon the study of effects, and drawing their conclusions from the outworking of these mistakes which the individuals have made and continue to make. No one who has awakened spiritually, and is seeing his three-fold being in the light of Truth, would speak of disease as something of itself. He would not think for a moment that the mind was fixed in old race beliefs or errors, not that his body was unresponsive to the Spirit.

And, so, we are asking you to deliberately turn from the doctors' opinions and verdict. And cease to even think the name they gave to the condition which existed in you at the time of their examination and treatment. Cast out and forget their assumption that this condition would not be changed and done away with utterly, just as you would refuse to hold and to think of some unworthy and untrue thing you might hear spoken as you walked down the street. Then, begin at once to rejoice that you are the offspring of God. That your life and substance of your body, and the perfect pattern of that life and body, are gifts of God—gifts which are in reality inseparably one with His own being, the very essence of God-Life and God-Substance and God-Intelligence. It is God's plan you know, to have the Creation picture forth, express, His own Ideas, qualities, and being. And it is our purpose in being here, to become conscious of and to express the true pattern and qualities of the Father-Mother.

We know very well that god would not create a man with imperfections and shortcomings and diseased conditions. But we know, also, that He would not create automatons, who were without free-will and the privilege of exercising their powers of son-ship. Just as we give our children, in our own thoughts of them, and our endeavors to live as we should that they may come forth clothed perfectly, the best that we can conceive, and then permit them to unfold their powers and faculties and their body-temples, as the inner intelligence and life prompts. We give them the best instruction we have to offer, of course; but if we are wise, we permit the Spirit within them to develop the soul, that it may express the individual gifts. So, we are accepting the God-given perfection, for you. And we are waiving aside the past mistakes, the untrue suggestions, and fixing undivided attention upon the Creator, and the inner pattern of perfection. This is the success of spiritual treatment. We bring all the mental attitudes, and the centers of consciousness, and even the physical structures to this high place in mind, where we see as God sees, and where we name all that is within us according to the patterns and uses for which these soul qualities and their out-picturings have been created.

Then, we prayerfully consider all our living habits, to get a better understanding of their purposes, and t know whether or not they are really chording with the divine law of health. We consider whether or not we are worrying, or fearing anything. We look back of the conscious mind, into the realm of the subconscious, or memory, to determine whether there is anything which took place in the past, to be continuing its disturbing influence through the unconscious expressions of mind. Much of the habit side of life is made up of these past experiences and trainings. Many things we do daily are not consciously thought out—are but the continuation of something impressed upon us long ago. We set to work to change any and everything which we may find that does not measure up to the best that our new light shows us. We know that it is of much more importance to change and to do that which is really best for our progress and our health, than to be smugly consistent, or to make the excuse that we have always done a thing and that it is too late to change now. The moment we discover something undesirable in our minds or our lives, we should seek to make the changes necessary to bring the desirable.

Mrs. Walker spoke of diet, which is one of these living habits which most of us have formed in ignorance of what is really best for us. We find that in most all so-called chronic disturbances or cases of long standing illnesses, there is need for changing some of the living habits, and diet is usually one of them. We not only have not known how to think right, but we have not learned to supply the body with what it requires to keep up all of its functioning. Habitual neglect, or failure to supply some of the required food elements, or indulgence in some of the things not needed, will overwork the digestive organs and the blood stream, and after a time there are evidences that some of these most important parts of the body are breaking down, or congesting, or weakening. Now, when such indications become known, the individual should surely love his own members enough to consider their problems and needs, and to do his part in supplying the needs.

This is where others who have made careful and prayerful study of the mental, and the physical construction of man, and of his needs, can help. We offer help through spiritual ideas, introduced into the every-day thinking, and the actions of the individual. There are others, who giving themselves to the more physical phase of instruction and healing. We here individually study out the needs of the body man, and supply them. But we cannot give time and space to the necessary directions for others' treatment and the helps in changing living habits, and especially diet. So, we refer them to those who are prepared to help in this field.

We have a splendid friend and co-worker out in Kansas, just now in Holton, who combines our method of treatment and instruction with this instruction and treatment through proper feeding, of which we have just spoken. We are glad to give you her address, that you may communicate with her, and if possible make arrangements with her to come to you for a time, to help you with your study and the selection and preparation of your foods. She is having great success in her work, and we know you will like her and be greatly benefited by what she has to give. Mrs. Emma E. Teter, just now, is at Mrs. Noda Wilson's home, 125 Iowa St., Holton, Kans. You may secure splendid little books, giving very simple and complete explanations of the benefits of the right uses of foods, and outlines showing just what each food is for, and how you may use it. You will find that our Dr. Beng. G. Hauser will give you a very pleasing and satisfying arrangement of meals, and that you will be very happy to take his treatment. Your entire blood stream will be quickly renewed, and you will become a new creature in flesh, as well as in mind. And the old conditions—you won't even remember them!

Mrs. Walker spoke of how nice it would be for you to come here. I truly believe it would be best for you to get in touch with Mrs. Teters, and have her in your home or near you for a few days or weeks, to help you with the new line of constructive thinking, and the right eating. Then, visit here, for closer touch with us, and some of the class work would be a delight to you, and you would be ready to take that which we may have for you. We have a splendid vegetarian cafeteria here, in the same block with the main Unity Buildings. You could eat there, and get the best of foods; but there is no special help in the selection of just what you most need. After you learn to select, then you could eat at the Inn, and your meals would be even more delicious and satisfying.

We are praying for you, and with you. We are inclosing herewith a special cleansing and healing prayer for you, and the regular monthly Class Thoughts which we use as the foundation of our studies and prayers. We are asking you to consider these little printed slips—not as they seem—but as the answers to prayers which we have united in holding, that God would give us the light and the words for realizing it, which would best meet the needs of humanity at the present time. Study the words, and the ideas conveyed by them, prayerfully; and then unite with us in declaring their Truth for yourself, and for others, and you will surely come into a fuller realization of God's presence and love and power and life in all his children and in all their affairs.

*Yours in Love and Truth,*

# Appendix Two

The healing power of the divine within became clear to Myrtle in two other important dreams.

## Dream One

*She described the context in which this dream occurred:*

For some days I had not been my usual self, and finally I had to go to bed. The world would say I was sick, dangerously ill, but I knew better. The truth was that I had allowed some thought of negation to creep into my consciousness, and that thought was inhibiting the free flow of God's perfect health in my body. I knew that just as soon as I replaced that negative thought with the realization of "God is my health, I can't be sick. I should be well." With this thought I went to sleep.

## Dream Two

*In a second dream she met a beautiful woman with whom she had a conversation. She reported:*

The sky was so blue and the fields were so green, and the flowers everywhere—I can't tell you how beautiful it was—just like dream! As I walked down the road, I met a beautiful woman dressed in a pure white robe with a gold girdle. She had wonderful golden hair and she smiled at me sweetly and said:

"How are you this fine day?"

"Very well," I faltered, " but can you tell me where I am?"

"Why, don't you know? You are in heaven."

I looked around in amazement. Then I looked at the woman, but I couldn't say a word. Then I thought of how as a little girl I had tried to imagine what heaven was like. I turned to the woman again and faltered. "Are you an angel?"

"Yes," she smiled "I'm an angel. Wouldn't you like to be one, too?"

"I suppose so," I replied, "but where 's God? I'd like to see Him."

"God! Why do you wish to see Him?"

Her question puzzled me. "Why would anyone want to see God!"

Still perplexed, I replied, "That's one reason why I wanted to come to heaven—to see Him."

"Did you think that you had come to heaven to find Him?"

"Well, I thought that I should find Him here. I was looking for Him when I met you, although I wasn't sure this was heaven."

"Where did you look?"

"Oh, I looked all about me! I thought that perhaps this road would take me to his place."

"Dear One," the angel said in a tone full of assurance. "He has no palace. He is all about you. He is here. He is with you now as He was on earth. But you will not find Him unless you look within yourself. At the center of y our being He abides forever. Turn within, and know that God is here."

The dream had a powerful impact because it awakened her with a start. She noticed how differently she felt about herself and about her connection with God.

I looked about me. Where was I. Why—I was in my own bed; but something was changed. Through my mind rang the words, "God is Here. God is here." I sat up exclaiming. "Yes, God is here, and in His presence I am well." I got up and dressed. When a friend came in a few moments later, she found me as well and strong as ever.

# Appendix Three

This is an affirmation which Myrtle Fillmore used when she was about to retire for the evening. I find it to be a particularly powerful statement of Truth, one which I use in my own practice.

*I am health, strength peace, happiness, prosperity.*

*The spirit of God flows through my body in a purifying, cleansing stream, removing all obstructions, bringing peace, health, and harmony to my body.*

*I am well, strong, vital—beautiful, peaceful, poised.*

*I am eternally youthful, I am buoyant, happy, free.*

*I shall rise in the morning filled with energy, radiance, and the power to accomplish whatever I find to do.*

# About the Author

Neal Vahle is the author of: *Open at the Top: The Life of Ernest Holmes*, Open View Press, 1993; *Torch-bearer to Light the Way: The Life of Myrtle Fillmore*, Open View Press, 1996; *The Unity Movement: Its Evolution and Spiritual Teaching*, Templeton Foundation Press, 2002; *Smart Baseball: How Professionals Play the Mental Game*, co-authored with Buddy Bell, St. Martin's Press, 2005; *The Spiritual Journey of Charles Fillmore: Discovering the Power Within*, Templeton Foundation Press, 2008; *A Course in Miracles: The Lives of Helen C. Schucman and William N. Thetford*, Open View Press, 2009; *Dr. Jack on Winning Basketball*, co-authored with Jack Ramsay, Blue River Press, 2011; *Eric Butterworth: His Life and Teaching*, Open View Press, 2012. Vahle served as editor of *World Affairs* journal 1969–1978), *New Realities* magazine (1986–1990), and *Unity Magazine* (2000–2005). He holds a doctorate in American History from Georgetown University. He was an adjunct professor of political science at American University; and an adjunct professor of American history at The Catholic University of America, and George Mason University. He served as executive director of Heldref Publications, Washington, DC. (1969–1990). He was a member of the Board of Directors, Unity School of Christianity, (2005–2008). He lives in San Francisco, California.

# *Endorsements*

This biography of Myrtle Fillmore is clear, objective, and very informative. It provides us with a new and deeper look at "the mother of Unity." It should be of great interest to anyone acquainted with the Unity movement, and particularly valuable to those of us who have been in Unity for a longer period of time.

> *Rev. Robert J. Brumet, M.S.*
> *Faculty, Spiritual Development and Pastoral Studies*
> *Unity Institute and Seminary*

Neal Vahle has captured Myrtle Fillmore's spirit and her extraordinary contribution to the renaissance of the ways of prayer and to the transformation of consciousness.

> *Rev. Sharon Connors, Christ Church Unity of El Cajon.*

In this insightful work, Neal Vahle opens the door to the heart and mind of Myrtle Fillmore, and shows us her faith and commitment to Spiritual Truth that birthed a worldwide movement.

> *Marge and Bill Dale, Unity ministers and retired vice-presidents*
> *and former members of the Board of Trustees of Unity School of Christianity.*

An inspiring and instructive account of one of the early pioneers of modern spirituality.

> *Rev. Justin Epstein, Author of Super You,*
> *and minister of The Unity Center of New York City*

Neal Vahle's historic literary work accurately and chronologically reports the life and loves of Myrtle Fillmore, the co-founder of Unity. It is steeped with a plethora of Myrtle's inspiring thoughts capturing the strength, class, healing power and mysticism of the woman who was the heart of the Unity Movement. Certainly thousands of hours were invested in compiling and writing this masterpiece of epic importance in recording Unity's history. Reading "Lighting the Way" is a consciousness raising experience!

> *John R. Knowles, CEO/Chairman of the Board, Plymouth Industries, Inc.,*
> *Member, Board of Directors, Unity School of Christianity;*
> *former minister/spiritual leader of Unity of Sheboygan Church*

Neal Vahle's wonderful new book about my grandmother's amazing journey, from darkness and despair into becoming a spiritual way-shower, is an inspiration to me. It will also inspire others involved with Unity, as well as many people around the world.

> *Rosemary Fillmore Rhea, Unity School of Christianity*

# *Myrtle Fillmore:*

In this new biography, Neal Vahle provides us with a fresh and expanded view of an amazing woman who was a tireless healing practitioner and teacher of Truth. This is a fascinating profile of a person who can arguably be considered one of the most influential women of the 19th and 20th century.

> *Michael Sheets, Member, Board of Directors, Unity School of Christianity*

Neal Vahle's new biography on Myrtle Fillmore is filled with fascinating information about this remarkable woman on every page. Anyone interested in the Unity movement, from long-time practitioners to new students of spiritual Truth, will be enlightened and entertained by this wonderful book. I especially appreciate knowing that our co-founder had her not-so-holy challenges that she, too, was working through in her life. This book doesn't gloss over the fact that we are all on the spiritual path and sometimes stumble in our journey; Neal powerfully reveals the real woman beneath the icon. I feel I know "Mama Myrtle" on a deeper level than ever before. I highly recommend this terrific book.

> *Rev. Paul Tenaglia, Unity of New York*

*Myrtle Fillmore: Lighting the Way* earns my highest recommendation. Neal Vahle presents the story of the woman whose faith and courage inspired the foundation of the Unity movement in an engaging narrative that will appeal to both casual readers and more serious students of Unity and New Thought. Through Vahle's summary of her spiritual teaching and practice, gathered primarily from her correspondence, readers will experience Myrtle Fillmore's practical mysticism as clearly and powerfully as did Unity students during Myrtle's lifetime. *Myrtle Fillmore: Lighting the Way* offers readers an experience of both the powerful spirituality and exquisite humanness of Unity's co-founder.

> *Rev. Tom Thorpe, faculty member, Unity Institute and Seminary*

*Myrtle Fillmore: Lighting the Way* is a fabulous book. Neal Vahle presents a very intimate picture of Myrtle as a person and a spiritual practitioner in such a way that after reading the book I felt as if she had been my lifelong friend. This should be on everybody's reading list.

> *Duke Tufty, Senior Minister of Unity Temple on the Plaza,*
> *and former chairman of the Board of Directors, Unity School of Christianity,*
> *Unity Worldwide Headquarters*

If you want to be inspired with the power of spiritual growth in action, Neal Vahle's biography of Myrtle Fillmore is for you. In this comprehensive account, we experience a woman, sick in body and destined to a short and limited life by her 19th century culture and upbringing, transformed into a healthy, vital, energetic and visionary co-founder of the Unity Movement. Vahle succeeds in showing us how this happens and brings us up close and personal to Myrtle's inner life with new and revealing details. You'll get to know her as never before. In his exhaustive chapter on her spiritual teaching, Vahle helps us see clearly the ideas that were driving Unity at that time—a great resource for New Thought and Unity students.

*Reverend Philip White, former editor of Unity Magazine*
*and dean of education for Unity School of Christianity*